THE PRAYER MANUAL

UNLOCKING THE POWER OF COMMUNICATION WITH GOD

TOM CORNELL

The Prayer Manual

Unlocking the Power of Communication with God

Tom Cornell

SOZO PUBLISHING

CONTENTS

Introduction

Unlocking the Power of Communication with God

Prayer is not a religious routine, a spiritual exercise, or a mystical ritual reserved for a few elite saints. Prayer is the breath of the believer. It is the open channel through which Heaven touches Earth and Earth responds to Heaven. It is the foundation of every move of God, the fuel of every victorious life, and the lifeline of every son and daughter who desires to walk closely with the Father.

In a time when busyness often replaces stillness and performance overshadows intimacy, the call to a deeper life of prayer is not just a suggestion—it is a divine summons. The power of prayer has been underestimated, misrepresented, and in many cases, abandoned. Yet every generation that has shaken nations, broken chains, and ushered in revival has rediscovered the ancient path of fervent, consistent, Spirit-led prayer.

This book is not written for the purpose of adding more information to your spiritual library. It is a manual—a practical and prophetic tool for unlocking the life-altering power of prayer in your personal walk with God, your leadership, your church, and your calling. It is meant to stir your spirit, confront apathy, and equip you to pray in a way that gets results.

Why Prayer Matters

There are many things that believers can do to build their spiritual life, but there is nothing that replaces the necessity of prayer. Prayer is the foundation that supports every other discipline. Without prayer, reading the Word can become intellectual; worship can become performance; service can become duty. But with prayer, everything becomes intimate. Everything becomes empowered.

Why does prayer matter so much? Because God has chosen prayer as the means by which His will is established on Earth. He has chosen to work through partnership with His people, not apart from them. Every breakthrough, every healing, every salvation, and every move of God in history can be traced back to someone who prayed. Men and women who refused to live in their own strength and cried out for Heaven's help—these are the ones who changed the course of families, cities, and nations.

Prayer matters because God responds to it. He listens. He moves. He answers. But more importantly, He reveals Himself. Prayer is not just about what we say or even what we get. It's about who we become in the process of seeking Him. When we pray, we align ourselves with Heaven. We exchange our weakness for His strength, our confusion for His wisdom, and our burdens for His peace.

Jesus: The Model of a Praying Life

The clearest picture of a life of prayer is found in the life of Jesus. He was not only a man of miracles and messages; He was a man of prayer. Before the crowds gathered, He prayed. Before the miracles multiplied, He withdrew to be alone with the Father. Before choosing the twelve, He spent all night in prayer. Before the cross, He prayed with blood and tears. And after the resurrection, He continues as our Great Intercessor, seated at the right hand of the Father, praying for us (Hebrews 7:25).

Jesus did not treat prayer as optional, nor did He rely on His divine nature to bypass the need for prayer. He showed us what it looks like to live fully dependent on the Father. If Jesus—fully God yet fully man—prioritized prayer, how much more must we?

He prayed in solitude, He prayed in community, He prayed in the early morning, and He prayed late at night. His life was saturated with prayer, not as a religious requirement, but as a rhythm of communion. He did not pray only to ask for things—He prayed to align, to receive, to surrender, and to abide.

Jesus taught His disciples to pray by example before He taught them with words. When they said, "Lord, teach us to pray," it was not because they didn't know prayers. It was because they saw something in His prayer life that they did not yet possess —power, peace, and intimacy. This book is written for the same reason. We want to move beyond prayer lists and empty phrases into a lifestyle of communion and authority.

Prayer as Communion

At its core, prayer is communion with God. It is conversation, connection, and companionship with the One who created us, redeemed us, and now lives within us. It is where hearts are opened, love is poured out, and transformation begins.

Communion is not rushed. It is not mechanical. It is not something we check off a list. Communion takes time. It takes attention. It takes heart. In communion, we are not just heard—we are held. We are not just talking—we are being changed.

The believer who sees prayer only as a place to make requests will miss the deeper reward of relationship. God is not a vending machine waiting for your correct code. He is a Father waiting for your face. He wants to talk to you, yes—but more than that, He wants to walk with you. In the cool of the day, in the fire of trial, in the ordinary routines—He desires communion.

Prayer as communion also means that we must learn to listen. True prayer is not one-sided. The most powerful moments in prayer are often the ones where we say nothing, and He speaks. When we learn to wait on Him, to linger in His presence, and to value His voice, we move into maturity. Prayer becomes less about our agenda and more about His heart.

Prayer as Partnership

Prayer is not only communion—it is partnership. God has chosen to rule the Earth through willing vessels. He has entrusted His authority to sons and daughters who will legislate from the secret place. Through prayer, we partner with the purposes of God to see His Kingdom come and His will be done.

This kind of partnership means we are not begging God to move—we are declaring His promises, enforcing His victory, and releasing His power. We pray not as orphans hoping for scraps, but as heirs releasing inheritance.

When Elijah prayed, it stopped raining. When Moses prayed, the sea parted. When Daniel prayed, angels moved. When the early church prayed, prison doors opened and the Spirit was poured out. This is partnership. God moves through those who move with Him.

In this manual, we will explore the different types of prayer that are part of this partnership—intercession, supplication, declaration, agreement, and more. Each has a distinct role in the work of the Kingdom. As we grow in understanding, we grow in effectiveness.

Prayer as Warfare

One of the most overlooked aspects of prayer is its role in spiritual warfare. Prayer is not only intimacy—it is also invasion. It is how we displace darkness, destroy demonic agendas, and push back against the gates of hell.

The enemy does not fear church attendance. He does not tremble at programs. But he fears prayer. Especially the prayer of a righteous believer who knows their authority. Prayer breaks strongholds. It binds and looses. It silences accusations and releases deliverance. It is the strategy of victory for every battle.

The believer who does not pray will be overwhelmed by warfare. But the believer who learns to war in prayer will walk in sustained victory. You were never called to live reactive—you were called to live offensive, standing in the authority of Christ and enforcing His dominion through prayer.

The prayers of the early church were not soft. They were bold, powerful, and effective. They shook buildings. They brought justice. They shifted history. This is the kind of prayer we are reclaiming—a prayer that fights not in the flesh, but in the Spirit.

What You Can Expect From This Manual

This book is divided into four parts:

- Part One lays the foundation, helping you understand what prayer truly is, why it's essential, and what can hinder its effectiveness. These chapters are meant to deepen your hunger and clarify your understanding.
- Part Two explores the different types of prayer found in Scripture. Each chapter unpacks the purpose, practice, and biblical pattern for these expressions— adoration, thanksgiving, confession, supplication, intercession, and more.
- Part Three equips you with practical tools to build a strong, consistent prayer life. We'll talk about forming habits, incorporating fasting, praying in the Spirit, and using the Word in prayer.
- Part Four focuses on prayer's role in the advancement of the Kingdom. We'll discuss revival prayer, building prayer movements, and raising up others in a lifestyle of prayer.

This manual is not a rulebook—it is a guide to deeper relationship and greater impact. Whether you are just beginning your prayer journey or are a seasoned intercessor, this book will challenge you to go higher, dig deeper, and believe for more.

A Call to the Secret Place

If we are going to see the kind of Kingdom breakthrough that our families, churches, cities, and nations desperately need, we must return to the secret place. We must rebuild the altar of prayer—personally and corporately. We must stop depending on talent, strategy, and performance, and start crying out for presence, power, and purpose.

God is looking for those who will stand in the gap, who will weep between the porch and the altar, who will birth revival through prayer. He is looking for those who will not just talk about prayer but live it—who will be burning ones, watchmen, and lovers of His presence. This is your invitation. Not just to read—but to respond. Not just to learn—but to burn.

Welcome to The Prayer Manual. Let us journey together into the presence of God, into the authority of the Spirit, and into a life of prayer that changes everything.

CHAPTER 1

WHAT IS PRAYER?

Prayer is the most vital spiritual discipline in the life of a believer, yet it is often the most misunderstood and neglected. Many approach prayer as if it were merely a means to an end—something we do to get what we want from God. Others avoid it altogether, convinced that prayer is complicated, ineffective, or reserved only for the "spiritually elite." But prayer is not for the elite; it is the inheritance of every child of God. Prayer is not meant to be rare or ritualistic; it is intended to be relational and regular.

Before we can explore how to pray effectively, we must first answer the foundational question: What is prayer? The answer to this question is not found in formulas or traditions, but in the very heart of God. Prayer is not man reaching for the divine out of desperation; it is God inviting His sons and daughters into a divine conversation.

The Definition of Prayer

At its simplest, prayer is communication with God. It is both talking to God and listening to Him. It is the divine dialogue that happens between the Creator and His creation, between a Father and His children. Prayer is not simply words uttered into the air —it is spirit-to-Spirit communication that touches Heaven and transforms Earth.

The Hebrew word for prayer, tefillah, and the Greek word proseuchomai, both imply not just speaking, but devotion, connection, and worship. Prayer involves both reverence and relationship. It carries the weight of communion and the intensity of intercession. It is the heart laid bare before God and the spirit lifted high in His presence.

Prayer is multifaceted. It can be intimate or intense, whispered or shouted, solitary or corporate. It may look like silence soaked in tears, or it may sound like declarations of spiritual authority. But regardless of the expression, true prayer is always about connection. Without connection, prayer becomes a religious form. With connection, it becomes a life-giving force.

Prayer is not transactional; it is transformational. It is not just about presenting our requests but about being shaped in the process. It's about aligning with God's will, surrendering our agenda, and learning to carry His heart.

Prayer as Relationship, Not Ritual

One of the greatest tragedies in the church today is that prayer has been reduced to a formula—something mechanical rather than relational. Many believers feel pressure to "pray right," as if God only listens to polished prayers filled with perfect words. But God is not impressed with performance. He is moved by authenticity. He does not require eloquence—He desires engagement.

Jesus made this clear when He warned against prayers that were filled with vain repetition (Matthew 6:7). He was not saying repetition is wrong—He Himself repeated prayers in the garden of Gethsemane—but rather, He condemned prayers that lacked heart, substance, and relationship. The Pharisees prayed to be seen by men; Jesus prayed to be with the Father.

When we understand prayer as relationship, everything changes. We stop striving to say the "right thing," and we begin leaning into the reality that God wants us—our presence, our honesty, our time. Prayer becomes less about getting answers and more about knowing the Answerer.

Relationships thrive on communication. A marriage without conversation withers. A friendship without connection fades. So it is with our relationship with God. Prayer is the oxygen of our intimacy with Him. When we stop praying, we suffocate our spiritual life. But when we prioritize communion, we flourish in His presence.

This is why Jesus retreated to pray so often. Not because He needed to check off a spiritual task, but because He needed the voice of the Father more than the applause of men. He lived in such deep dependence that He could say, "I only do what I see My Father doing" (John 5:19). This clarity came from the place of prayer.

Prayer in the Old Testament

To fully understand what prayer is, we must trace its thread throughout Scripture. From Genesis to Malachi, the Old Testament reveals a pattern of men and women who walked with God through prayer.

In Genesis, we see the first picture of divine communion as Adam walked with God in the cool of the day. Though the word "prayer" is not used, the picture is clear—God's desire has always been fellowship. Sin fractured this communion, but from that moment on, God pursued humanity through relationship, and prayer became the bridge between broken man and a holy God.

Abraham, known as a friend of God, interceded for Sodom and Gomorrah, bargaining with God on behalf of a city. Moses spoke to God face to face as a man speaks to his friend, receiving instruction, wisdom, and intervention for Israel. David poured out his heart in songs and cries, writing prayers that still guide believers today.

The Old Testament shows us that prayer was not bound to temples or rituals. Though systems were put in place, the heart of prayer was always relational. Hannah prayed in anguish. Elijah prayed for fire. Daniel prayed with discipline and boldness. These men and women understood that prayer could move Heaven and shift history.

But their prayers were not magic—they were birthed in relationship. They knew who they were talking to. They knew His voice, His nature, His covenant. That intimacy made their prayers powerful.

Prayer in the New Testament

In the New Testament, the full expression of prayer is revealed in the person of Jesus and the outpouring of the Holy Spirit. Prayer is no longer confined to the temple—it becomes the temple. We, as believers, become the dwelling place of God, and prayer flows from the heart of the redeemed.

Jesus did not only teach His disciples how to pray—He modeled a lifestyle of prayer. He began His ministry in prayer, continued it in prayer, and finished it in prayer. He often withdrew to lonely places to seek the Father, showing us that power in public is always preceded by prayer in private.

In Luke 11, when the disciples asked, "Lord, teach us to pray," Jesus responded with what we now call the Lord's Prayer. This was not meant to be a rigid formula but a framework—a pattern to guide us into relational communion. It begins with "Our Father," immediately rooting prayer in identity and relationship, not ritual.

The book of Acts shows us that the early church was born in prayer, sustained in prayer, and multiplied through prayer. From the upper room to the prison cell, prayer was the consistent theme. They prayed in tongues, they prayed for boldness, they prayed for miracles—and Heaven responded.

Paul, in his letters, urged believers to "pray without ceasing," to make prayer a continual part of their lives. He described prayer as a weapon, a form of spiritual warfare that tears down strongholds (2 Corinthians 10:4). He taught that we could pray in the Spirit, sing in prayer, intercede with groans too deep for words, and partner with the will of God through prayer.

The New Testament reveals that prayer is not just something we do—it's who we are. It is the breath of our spiritual life and the foundation of Kingdom advancement.

Prayer Is a Place of Encounter

Prayer is not just about speaking—it's about encountering. It's about meeting with God and being changed by His presence. The secret place is not just a metaphor; it is a spiritual reality. Jesus said, "When you pray, go into your room and shut the door..." (Matthew 6:6). That place of intimacy becomes a place of transformation.

Many believers treat prayer like a duty. But when you encounter God in prayer, it becomes a delight. It becomes the place where fears are broken, direction is received, healing is released, and joy is restored. Prayer becomes the source, not the side dish. It becomes the engine, not the emergency brake.

The question is not, "Do you pray?" The real question is, "Do you meet God when you pray?" When Moses met with God on the mountain, his face shone. When Isaiah saw the Lord in the temple, he was undone. When Paul encountered Jesus on the road, his entire direction changed. Prayer is the pathway to divine encounter.

Prayer Is the Heartbeat of Revival

Every move of God throughout history was birthed in prayer. Whether it was the Moravian prayer movement, the Welsh Revival, the Azusa Street outpouring, or the Jesus Movement— none of it happened without prayer. When prayer rooms burn, revival spreads. When altars are rebuilt, the fire falls.

This is not coincidental. It is divine design. God moves where He is welcomed. He fills the space that has been prepared. And prayer prepares the way. It plows the ground. It tears down resistance and opens the heavens.

If we want to see revival in our homes, cities, and nations, we must return to the place of prayer. Not passive prayer. Not polished prayer. Prevailing prayer. Prophetic prayer. Persistent prayer. Prayer that doesn't let go until Heaven touches Earth.

Rediscovering the Essence of Prayer

So, what is prayer? Prayer is communion with the Father, alignment with His will, and partnership with His purposes. It is a divine invitation to know Him, to walk with Him, and to carry His heart into the world. It is not a ritual to be performed but a relationship to be cultivated.

When prayer becomes central, everything else comes into alignment. Identity is strengthened. Vision is clarified. Power is released. Discernment increases. Intimacy deepens. And we begin to live, not by natural sight, but by the whisper of Heaven.

This is the kind of prayer this manual is designed to stir within you—not just informational prayer, but transformational prayer. Not just praying for results, but praying for relationship. As we continue through this journey, remember this:

Prayer is not something you master; it's someone you meet. Let's go deeper. Let's learn, not just how to pray—but how to live a praying life.

Activation

Find a quiet space. Ask the Holy Spirit to make you aware of His nearness. Spend ten minutes simply talking to God as Father—no requests, only conversation. Record what you sense.

Discussion Questions

1. The book calls prayer *"the breath of the believer"*—the lifeline of every son and daughter of God. In what ways does neglecting prayer suffocate spiritual life, and how can consistent communion with God restore vitality and clarity of purpose?

2. Scripture shows that *God has chosen to work through partnership with His people, not apart from them.* How does this truth reshape your understanding of divine sovereignty and human responsibility? What would change in your prayer life if you truly believed Heaven is waiting for your agreement?

3. *"Prayer is not just about what we say or what we get—it's about who we become."* Reflect on a season where prayer didn't immediately change your situation but changed you. What does that reveal about God's ultimate goal in prayer—transformation or transaction?

CHAPTER 2

THE PURPOSE OF PRAYER

Before you can master something, you must understand its purpose. Misunderstanding purpose leads to misuse, abuse, or neglect. The same is true of prayer. When believers do not grasp why prayer matters, they either avoid it entirely or engage in it from a place of obligation rather than revelation. But when the true purpose of prayer is revealed, prayer becomes irresistible—it becomes the heartbeat of a life aligned with God.

Prayer is not primarily about getting something from God. It is about getting to God. It is not just about asking for help in a crisis, but about living in daily partnership with Heaven. It is not about bending God's will to our own—it is about surrendering to His and seeing His Kingdom manifest on the Earth.

In this chapter, we will explore three foundational purposes of prayer: intimacy with God, partnering with Heaven to bring change, and building spiritual strength and sensitivity. When these are understood and embraced, prayer becomes more than a spiritual activity—it becomes a lifestyle that shapes who you are and what you carry.

1. Intimacy with God

At the core of all prayer is this: God wants to be known. He is not a distant deity, demanding homage from afar. He is a loving Father who desires relationship with His children. Every call to prayer in Scripture is ultimately a call to deeper intimacy.

The first and highest purpose of prayer is not intercession, warfare, or requests—it is communion. In the Garden of Eden, God walked with Adam. That was the original design—unbroken fellowship between God and man. Sin disrupted that connection, but through Christ, the veil was torn and the invitation to communion was restored.

The prophet Hosea carried the cry of God's heart when he wrote, "I desire mercy, not sacrifice, and acknowledgment of God rather than burnt offerings" (Hosea 6:6). In other words, God wants hearts, not just habits. He desires nearness, not performance.

Jesus reinforced this when He called His disciples not servants, but friends. Servants receive commands. Friends receive intimacy. When we pray, we are not just speaking to a sovereign King—we are communing with our heavenly Father.

The secret place becomes sacred not because of its location, but because of the Person we meet there. Time in prayer is not a duty but a delight when it is centered on the pursuit of God Himself. When Moses prayed, "Show me Your glory," he wasn't asking for provision or victory—he was asking for God's presence. That is the essence of intimacy.

David, the man after God's heart, expressed this longing in Psalm 27:4—"One thing I ask from the Lord... that I may dwell in the house of the Lord all the days of my life." Prayer was not

David's occasional activity; it was his dwelling place. He didn't want to just visit God—he wanted to live with Him.

Prayer builds intimacy because it creates space for conversation. Just as relationships grow through communication, so our relationship with God grows through prayer. When we listen, when we linger, when we speak honestly and wait patiently, our hearts become aligned with His.

The enemy knows this, which is why he fights to keep you busy, distracted, or spiritually numb. He knows that a praying believer is a connected believer, and a connected believer is a powerful one. Your effectiveness in the Kingdom will never exceed your intimacy with the King.

2. Partnering with Heaven to Bring Change

Prayer is not just communion—it is commission. It is how sons and daughters partner with Heaven to enforce God's will on the Earth. Jesus taught His disciples to pray, "Your Kingdom come, Your will be done, on earth as it is in Heaven." That is not a poetic phrase—it is a governmental mandate.

God has chosen to accomplish much of His work on Earth in partnership with people. He could do it all sovereignly, but He invites us to co-labor with Him through prayer. Prayer is how we legislate in the spirit, how we release Heaven's agenda, and how we enforce Christ's victory over the powers of darkness.

This is what gives intercession such weight. When Abraham prayed for Sodom, he wasn't just appealing for mercy—he was stepping into governmental authority. When Elijah prayed for rain to stop, and then again for it to start, he wasn't manipulating the weather—he was standing in alignment with Heaven's purpose and acting as a prophetic gatekeeper over the land.

In the New Testament, we see this partnership in action repeatedly. The early church prayed, and prison doors opened. They prayed, and the Holy Spirit descended. They prayed, and boldness filled the room. These weren't polite prayers—they were powerful decrees rooted in a deep understanding of spiritual authority.

Too often, modern believers pray as if they are powerless—hoping that maybe God will do something. But true prayer is not passive. It is assertive, aligned, and authoritative. Jesus said, "Whatever you bind on earth will be bound in Heaven, and whatever you loose on earth will be loosed in Heaven" (Matthew 18:18). This language is judicial. It implies that in prayer, we are not simply beggars—we are legislators.

When we pray according to God's will, as revealed in His Word and by His Spirit, we step into divine partnership. We become conduits of breakthrough. Angels respond. Chains break. Strongholds collapse. Territories shift.

This kind of prayer requires discernment. It is not about praying for our comfort—it is about praying for Kingdom advancement. When we ask God what He desires, and then echo that back to Him in bold faith, we are partnering with Him to bring change in our families, churches, cities, and nations.

Prayer is how the Kingdom invades the chaos of the world. And you are not just invited to participate—you are needed.

3. Building Spiritual Strength and Sensitivity

The third foundational purpose of prayer is personal transformation. Prayer is not just about changing the world around you—it's about changing the world within you. When you pray, you grow. When you pray consistently, you mature.

Prayer develops spiritual strength. Just as the body needs consistent nourishment and exercise to stay strong, so your spirit needs the discipline of prayer to remain healthy. A prayerless believer is a weak believer, vulnerable to temptation, confusion, and spiritual lethargy. But a praying believer is alert, sharp, and anchored.

Jude 20 says, "But you, beloved, building yourselves up in your most holy faith and praying in the Holy Spirit..." Prayer builds. It strengthens. It stretches. It awakens dormant faith and reignites spiritual fire.

There are many believers who want to walk in power but are unwilling to cultivate consistency. They want anointing without altar time. But the principle remains: power in public flows from prayer in private.

Jesus demonstrated this. Before choosing His disciples, He prayed all night. Before miracles, He withdrew. His power was not random—it was the result of disciplined intimacy. He modeled what it meant to live spiritually strong, fully attuned to the Father.

Prayer also develops spiritual sensitivity. When you pray, especially when you wait and listen, your spiritual senses are trained. You begin to discern God's voice more clearly. You become aware of the nudges of the Holy Spirit. You sense spiritual atmospheres. You perceive demonic resistance. You gain prophetic insight into the times and seasons.

Romans 12:2 says that transformation comes by the renewing of the mind. Prayer is one of the primary ways our mind is renewed and our spirit attuned. In prayer, wrong thinking is confronted. In prayer, lies are replaced with truth. In prayer, burdens are lifted and clarity comes.

This is why the enemy works overtime to keep you out of prayer. Because if you ever become spiritually strong and sensitive, you become dangerous to the kingdom of darkness. You start hearing strategies from Heaven. You start walking in peace that makes no sense. You start praying with power that releases healing and deliverance.

Prayer is not a spiritual luxury. It is a necessity. It is the gymnasium of the spirit, the classroom of revelation, and the incubator of Kingdom identity. You cannot live in victory if you live without prayer.

The Three Purposes in Harmony

Each of these purposes of prayer—intimacy, partnership, and strength—work in harmony. You cannot truly partner with God unless you first know Him intimately. You cannot sustain partnership unless you are spiritually strong. You cannot grow strong unless you remain in communion.

Prayer is the convergence point of relationship, responsibility, and revelation. It is where we know God, work with God, and are changed by God.

It is important not to elevate one purpose at the expense of the others. Some believers focus only on intimacy and never step into authority. Others focus only on warfare and neglect the place of stillness. True maturity in prayer is learning to flow in all dimensions as the Spirit leads.

In one moment, you may be worshipping in adoration. In the next, you may be weeping in intercession. In another, you may be quietly listening. Each form of prayer fulfills a purpose, and each draws you deeper into the life of the Spirit.

The Fruit of Praying with Purpose

When you understand the purpose of prayer and begin to pray from that revelation, the fruit in your life will be undeniable:

- Greater intimacy with God. You will begin to sense His presence more tangibly, hear His voice more clearly, and carry His heart more consistently.
- Increased authority in the Spirit. Your prayers will shift from begging to declaring. You will start seeing real breakthrough as you align with Heaven.
- Personal transformation. Old patterns will begin to break. Fear will give way to faith. Your desires will begin to reflect God's desires. You'll be more sensitive to the Spirit's leading and more resistant to the enemy's lies.
- Clarity of purpose. As you pray, vision sharpens. Confusion lifts. Identity becomes solidified. You begin to walk with divine confidence and spiritual discernment.

This is the fruit of prayer rooted in purpose—not random, ritualistic prayer, but Spirit-led, purpose-driven prayer.

Pray On Purpose

To pray without understanding purpose is to miss the power of prayer. But to pray with revelation of its purpose is to step into a divine rhythm that transforms everything.

God is not calling you to pray more out of guilt or pressure. He is inviting you into deeper purpose. He is calling you to walk with Him, work with Him, and be shaped by Him. This is the invitation to a life of purpose-filled prayer.

So as you move forward in this manual, let this be your foundation:

- Pray to know Him.
- Pray to partner with Him.
- Pray to be shaped by Him.

In the next chapter, we'll look at the hindrances that often block our prayers—and how to overcome them. Because once you understand the purpose of prayer, the next step is to protect that purpose from sabotage.

Until then, pray on purpose.

Activation

Write three sentences that begin with "I pray to ..."—one for knowing Him, one for partnering with Him, one for being shaped by Him. Pray them aloud each morning this week.

Discussion Questions

1. *Prayer exists to build intimacy, release partnership, and develop spiritual strength.* Which of these purposes—intimacy, partnership, or strength—needs renewal in your life, and what might that look like practically?

2. How does understanding prayer as alignment with Heaven shift your motives when you approach God?

3. If the true purpose of prayer is transformation, not transaction, how would that redefine success in your prayer life?

CHAPTER 3

HINDRANCES TO EFFECTIVE PRAYER

It is one thing to know what prayer is and why it matters; it is another to deal honestly with the issues that block prayer from being effective. Just as a clogged artery restricts blood flow, so spiritual blockages can hinder the flow of God's presence, power, and voice in the life of a believer. Many Christians are praying, but not seeing results. They cry out to God, but feel as if their words fall to the ground. They attend prayer meetings, fast, and read the Word—but something seems off. Could it be that their prayers are hindered?

Scripture is clear: not all prayer is effective prayer. James 5:16 says, "The effective, fervent prayer of a righteous man avails much." This implies that prayer can also be ineffective, distracted, and powerless. If we want to walk in the kind of prayer life that produces results, we must be willing to deal with the hindrances.

This chapter will expose six of the most common hindrances to effective prayer: unforgiveness, unbelief, disobedience, busyness, distraction, and spiritual warfare. Each one of these functions as a spiritual barrier that must be torn down if we are to pray with clarity, authority, and results.

1. Unforgiveness: The Blockade of the Heart

Jesus made it clear that forgiveness is non-negotiable for those who follow Him. In the Lord's Prayer, He taught us to pray, "Forgive us our debts as we forgive our debtors" (Matthew 6:12). Then He added this sharp statement: "If you do not forgive others, your Father will not forgive your sins" (v. 15). Unforgiveness is not just a heart issue—it's a spiritual blockade.

When we refuse to forgive others, we build a wall between ourselves and God. Not because He is unwilling to speak, but because our hearts become closed off to His voice. Bitterness, offense, and resentment harden our spiritual sensitivity and pollute the atmosphere of our inner life.

Unforgiveness also disrupts the authority of our prayers. Jesus said that when we stand praying, if we remember someone we haven't forgiven, we must forgive them before continuing (Mark 11:25). Why? Because unforgiveness defiles our prayers. It introduces flesh into the Spirit. It mixes poison with purity.

If your prayer life feels stuck, ask the Holy Spirit to examine your heart. Is there someone you have not forgiven? A wound you've buried? An offense you've justified? Unforgiveness is not worth forfeiting fellowship with God. Release it. Forgive quickly. Let mercy triumph over judgment.

Forgiveness doesn't mean you condone what happened—it means you release it to God and trust Him to deal with it justly. It means you choose freedom over bondage and obedience over offense. It clears the atmosphere so Heaven can move freely in and through you.

2. Unbelief: The Poison of the Mind

Faith is the fuel of effective prayer. Hebrews 11:6 declares, "Without faith it is impossible to please God, because anyone who comes to Him must believe that He exists and that He rewards those who earnestly seek Him." When faith is absent, prayer becomes religious noise. When faith is present, prayer becomes prophetic force.

Unbelief is more than a feeling—it's a mindset. It is a spiritual condition that limits God's activity in your life. Jesus could not do many miracles in Nazareth because of the people's unbelief (Matthew 13:58). That's a sobering truth. Unbelief shuts down the supernatural. It causes us to pray small, safe prayers that require no faith and produce no results.

Many believers struggle with unbelief and don't even realize it. They go through the motions of prayer, but inwardly they doubt God's willingness, God's timing, or God's power. Some doubt that He even hears. Others believe He hears, but they assume He won't act. This hidden unbelief becomes a veil that clouds spiritual perception and limits breakthrough.

Faith, on the other hand, releases Heaven. Faith says, "I believe God is who He says He is, and He will do what He said He would do." Faith doesn't deny reality, but it elevates God's truth above circumstances. It fuels persistence, ignites boldness, and activates supernatural intervention.

If you want to grow in effective prayer, you must starve unbelief. Feed your spirit with the Word. Surround yourself with testimonies of answered prayer. Declare God's promises aloud until your soul catches up with your spirit. Faith comes by hearing—and that includes hearing yourself pray with expectation.

3. Disobedience: The Breach in Alignment

Disobedience may be the most underestimated hindrance to prayer in the Church. Many want the power of prayer without the purity it requires. But Scripture is clear: rebellion and compromise will hinder your ability to hear from God and release His authority.

Proverbs 28:9 says, "If anyone turns a deaf ear to the law, even his prayers are detestable." Psalm 66:18 says, "If I had cherished sin in my heart, the Lord would not have listened." These verses are not condemning—they are clarifying. God is not looking for perfect people, but He is looking for surrendered people.

When we walk in willful sin, we disrupt the flow of prayer. It's not that God becomes angry and storms off—it's that we place ourselves out of alignment. Authority flows from alignment. And alignment comes through obedience.

Obedience is not just about avoiding sin; it's about submitting to God's will. There are times when disobedience looks like delay. God speaks, and we hesitate. He prompts, and we ignore. He leads, and we resist. Every time we say "no" to the Spirit, we dull our sensitivity and forfeit spiritual authority.

If your prayers feel hollow, examine your obedience. Is there a command you've ignored? A conviction you've dismissed? A calling you've postponed? Obedience unlocks authority. And obedience is not just an event—it's a lifestyle. As we walk in holiness, humility, and surrender, our prayers become sharp, weighty, and heaven-backed.

4. Busyness: The Theft of Priority

One of the greatest weapons the enemy uses to hinder prayer is not sin—but schedule. He knows he cannot stop you from being saved, so he works to keep you distracted. He fills your life with demands, noise, and activities until there's no room for prayer. And when prayer is no longer prioritized, power leaks.

Jesus said, "Seek first the Kingdom of God..." (Matthew 6:33). First. Not last. Not if there's time. First. This is not just about order—it's about priority. Whatever comes first shapes everything that follows. If we start our day with prayer, we anchor our soul in truth before we face the chaos of life. If we postpone prayer until we're exhausted, we have already lost the battle for intimacy.

Busyness is often a disguise for spiritual drift. It numbs our sensitivity and weakens our urgency. It gives us a false sense of productivity while we neglect the most important thing: time with God. Like Martha in Luke 10, we become distracted by good things and miss the one thing that matters most—sitting at Jesus' feet.

The remedy is simple but costly: we must rearrange our lives around prayer. Not fit prayer into our life—build our life around it. Make room. Say no to lesser things. Wake up earlier. Shut off the noise. Fight for margin. If prayer isn't scheduled, it won't happen. And if it doesn't happen, everything else suffers.

You are not too busy to pray—you are too busy not to pray. Prayer doesn't waste time; it redeems it. When you give God your time, He gives you grace, wisdom, and strategy for everything else.

5. Distraction: The War for Attention

If busyness steals your time, distraction steals your focus. In a digital age filled with alerts, noise, and notifications, the ability to focus in prayer is under assault. Even when we try to pray, our minds race, our phones buzz, and our attention drifts. We start praying and end up checking emails. We begin worshiping and end up worrying.

Distraction is more than inconvenience—it's warfare. It's the enemy's attempt to keep you shallow, surface-level, and spiritually dull. Because he knows that the deeper you go in prayer, the more you hear, the more you see, and the more you carry.

To overcome distraction, you must be intentional. Shut off your devices. Turn off the noise. Create an environment of encounter. Have a designated space for prayer. Write down your thoughts if they're swirling. Pray the Word to stay grounded. Use worship to enter in.

Sometimes the greatest breakthrough in prayer comes after 20 minutes of pushing past mental clutter. Don't stop because you feel dry—press in until you break through. Make room for stillness. Don't rush. God doesn't shout to compete with your distractions—He waits for your attention.

Psalm 46:10 says, "Be still, and know that I am God." Stillness leads to knowing. And knowing leads to breakthrough.

6. Spiritual Warfare: The Battle in the Heavens

One of the least acknowledged hindrances to prayer is the reality of spiritual resistance. We are not just praying in a vacuum —we are praying into contested territory. The devil is not intimidated by prayerless Christians. But when you begin to pray in authority, in purity, and in the Spirit, resistance increases.

Daniel prayed for 21 days before the angel arrived with the answer. The delay was not due to sin, unbelief, or busyness—it was due to spiritual warfare (Daniel 10:12–13). A demonic principality resisted the answer in the heavenly realm. If Daniel had stopped praying on day 7 or day 15, he might never have seen the breakthrough.

This is why persistence in prayer matters. Just because you haven't seen results doesn't mean God hasn't heard. There may be warfare in the heavens. There may be a battle over your break-through. Don't quit. Don't let go. Don't stop pressing.

Sometimes the warfare increases right before the release. Discouragement is a sign the enemy fears your prayer. Delay is a sign something weighty is on the way. Keep declaring. Keep worshiping. Keep believing. When you pray, angels are dispatched, demons are confronted, and atmospheres shift—even if you don't see it right away.

Effective prayer is not just about how loud you are—it's about how long you're willing to stand. Stay in the fight. Breakthrough is often just beyond the point of giving up.

Tearing Down the Barriers

There is no condemnation for those in Christ Jesus—but there is conviction. And that conviction is a gift. It reveals what must be removed so that Heaven can move freely through your life.

If your prayers have felt stuck, ineffective, or dry, don't accept that as your normal. Ask the Holy Spirit to show you the hindrance. Is it unforgiveness? Unbelief? Disobedience? Busy-ness? Distraction? Spiritual warfare? Whatever it is, God's grace is available not just to reveal it—but to remove it.

You were created to pray with power. To walk in intimacy. To release Heaven on Earth. But that kind of prayer life doesn't happen automatically. It must be fought for, cultivated, and protected.

Tear down the barriers. Clear the clutter. Realign your heart. Reignite your faith.

The next chapter will take us deeper into the types of prayer, beginning with the prayer of adoration—because once the hindrances are removed, our hearts can rise again to worship the One who is worthy.

Now, let us pray—not hindered, but whole.

Activation

Ask the Holy Spirit to search your heart. Confess any unforgiveness or unbelief He reveals. Write a short "release" prayer declaring freedom from every hindrance.

Discussion Questions

1. *Barriers such as unbelief, disobedience, distraction, and unforgiveness weaken authority and intimacy.* Which hindrance most subtly undermines your consistency in prayer, and what truth from Scripture confronts it?

2. How does hidden offense or self-reliance close Heaven's flow, and what steps can reopen it?

3. When prayers seem unanswered, how can discernment reveal whether it's delay, denial, or divine redirection?

CHAPTER 4

THE PRAYER OF ADORATION

FOCUSING ON WHO GOD IS – DEVELOPING A HEART OF WORSHIP – EXAMPLES FROM THE PSALMS AND REVELATION

P rayer that transforms doesn't begin with asking—it begins with adoring. While supplication is necessary, and intercession powerful, the highest form of prayer is adoration. This is the kind of prayer that touches Heaven not because of what we need, but because of who God is. It doesn't seek His hand—it seeks His face. It doesn't start with a problem —it starts with praise.

The prayer of adoration is the kind of prayer that re-centers us. It lifts our gaze from ourselves to the throne. It breaks the cycle of self-focus and ushers us into the atmosphere of Heaven, where the angels cry "Holy, holy, holy" without ceasing. When we adore God, we join in Heaven's eternal chorus, not to get something, but simply because He is worthy.

In this chapter, we will explore the essence of adoration, how it realigns our heart, and why it is the foundation of every effective prayer life. We will look to Scripture—especially the Psalms and the book of Revelation—to see how the saints and angels modeled this kind of prayer. And finally, we will learn how to cultivate a lifestyle of adoration that births worship, intimacy, and awe.

1. Focusing on Who God Is

Adoration is the prayer that flows from the revelation of God's nature. It is the response of a heart that has seen the greatness, beauty, and holiness of the Lord. Where other types of prayer may center around our need, our calling, or our battle, adoration centers around His identity—His majesty, His mercy, His splendor.

The reason many believers struggle in prayer is because they begin in the wrong place. They begin with worry instead of worship, with anxiety instead of awe. But Jesus taught us to begin with adoration: "Our Father, who art in Heaven, hallowed be Thy name." Before petition, before confession, even before intercession—there is adoration.

To adore is to fix the eyes of your heart on the character of God. To speak back to Him what is true about Him. To behold His beauty, to magnify His name, and to love Him with your whole being. Adoration pulls us out of the chaos of life and into the stillness of glory.

When you begin your prayers with adoration, everything else comes into alignment. Your perspective changes. Your burdens shrink. Your spirit opens. You begin to sense the atmosphere of Heaven, where praise never stops and where God is always enough.

The enemy wants to pull your attention downward—to your needs, your failures, your disappointments. But adoration lifts your attention upward—to His faithfulness, His holiness, His consistency, and His unshakable throne.

2. Developing a Heart of Worship

The prayer of adoration is not just a technique; it's the fruit of a heart trained in worship. Worship is not a song—it is a posture. It is the deep internal recognition that God is worthy of everything: our time, our attention, our affection, our obedience.

A heart of worship is developed, not discovered. It is formed in the secret place. It is shaped through consistency, silence, and beholding. As you intentionally give God your attention—day after day—your heart begins to expand in love. You begin to long for His presence more than anything else.

Psalm 27:4 captures the essence of this desire: "One thing I ask from the Lord... that I may dwell in the house of the Lord all the days of my life, to gaze on the beauty of the Lord and to seek Him in His temple." This is adoration: gazing at God's beauty and being content just to be near Him.

A heart of worship doesn't need a reason to praise. It worships in the valley as well as on the mountaintop. It doesn't require breakthrough to adore—it adores because God is worthy, even if nothing changes.

Adoration is also deeply tied to the fear of the Lord. Not a fear that drives us away, but a holy reverence that draws us near. When we adore God, we are reminded that He is not like us—He is holy, infinite, glorious, and transcendent. Yet in His majesty, He draws close. This paradox—the God who is enthroned above the heavens yet lives within our hearts—fuels the fire of adoration.

3. Psalms: Adoration in the Heart of David

Nowhere in Scripture is the prayer of adoration more vividly modeled than in the Psalms. David, the man after God's own heart, understood how to adore. Whether in triumph or turmoil, he returned again and again to the posture of praise. Psalm 145 is a masterclass in adoration:

"I will exalt You, my God the King; I will praise Your name for ever and ever. Every day I will praise You and extol Your name for ever and ever. Great is the Lord and most worthy of praise; His greatness no one can fathom." (Psalm 145:1–3)

David begins not with his enemies or problems, but with God's greatness. He lifts God above every circumstance. He declares the goodness, mercy, faithfulness, and splendor of the Lord. His adoration is rich with imagery and soaked in awe.

This is not just poetic—it is powerful. Praise like this breaks chains. When David worshipped, demons fled from Saul. When the Levites praised at the temple, God's glory filled the room. Adoration brings the atmosphere of Heaven into the Earth.

Other Psalms reveal the same pattern:

- Psalm 29: *"Ascribe to the Lord the glory due His name; worship the Lord in the splendor of His holiness."*
- Psalm 63: *"Because Your love is better than life, my lips will glorify You."*
- Psalm 103: *"Bless the Lord, O my soul, and all that is within me, bless His holy name."*

David teaches us that adoration is not circumstantial—it is covenantal. It flows from who God is, not what we're experiencing. It is a decision to honor Him, even when life feels uncertain. It is a spiritual discipline that becomes a supernatural delight.

4. Revelation: Adoration in the Throne Room

While the Psalms give us the earthly expression of adoration, the book of Revelation gives us the heavenly model. In Revelation 4 and 5, John is caught up into the throne room of God. There, he sees living creatures, elders, and angels—all caught up in endless worship.

> *"Day and night they never stop saying:*
> *'Holy, holy, holy is the Lord God Almighty,*
> *who was, and is, and is to come.'"*
> *(Revelation 4:8)*

This is not boredom—it's burning. The living creatures are not singing out of duty, but out of unending discovery. Every time they behold God, they see something they've never seen before. And their response is adoration. In Revelation 5, the Lamb takes the scroll, and all of Heaven erupts:

> *"Worthy is the Lamb who was slain,*
> *to receive power and wealth and wisdom and strength*
> *and honor and glory and praise!"*
> *(Revelation 5:12)*

This is the language of adoration—praise focused entirely on the worthiness of the Lamb. Not one request. Not one complaint. Just exaltation. This throne room model should define our own prayer life. Before we ask, we adore. Before we fight, we bow. Before we declare, we gaze.

When you begin to adore God like this, your room becomes a throne room. The atmosphere changes. Your spirit aligns. Your prayers gain weight. Why? Because Heaven responds to the sound of adoration. It is the sound that fills God's courts. And when you echo that sound, you come into agreement with the reality of Heaven.

5. Cultivating a Lifestyle of Adoration

The prayer of adoration is not just for worship services —it is for daily life. You can adore God on your drive to work. In your living room. On a walk. In a prison cell. Adoration is not restricted by environment; it is awakened by attention.

Here are some practical ways to cultivate a lifestyle of adoration:

a. Start Your Prayer Time with Adoration

Before you make any request, spend time simply worshiping God. Thank Him for who He is—His holiness, His faithfulness, His mercy. Speak His names. Meditate on His character. Let your spirit magnify the Lord.

b. Pray the Psalms Out Loud

Use David's prayers to shape your own. Let the language of Scripture become the language of your heart. When you run out of words, borrow his. You'll find that your spirit begins to rise in worship.

c. Build a Worship Atmosphere

Use music to help cultivate adoration. Play instrumental worship or songs focused on God's nature. Sing if you can. Dance if you want. Do whatever draws your heart upward in reverence and delight.

d. Keep a "Who God Is" Journal

Write down every name, title, and attribute of God that you encounter in Scripture. Meditate on one each day. Let your adoration grow from revelation.

e. Let Creation Stir Your Wonder

Take walks. Gaze at the stars. Watch the ocean. Let nature preach to your soul. All of creation echoes God's majesty—and adoration is the proper response.

6. The Power and Fruit of Adoration

When you pray the prayer of adoration consistently, it will change you. You will begin to walk with awe. Your perspective will shift. Your burdens will feel lighter. Your intimacy with God will deepen. Here are just a few of the fruits of adoration:

- Humility: You realize how great He is, and how small your worries are.
- Joy: In His presence is fullness of joy.
- Clarity: Adoration silences confusion and brings divine perspective.
- Sensitivity: Your heart becomes more tender, more aware of His nearness.
- Authority: Praise clears the atmosphere for breakthrough to manifest.

Most importantly, adoration builds a relationship. It deepens love. It draws you close. It reminds you that you were made not just to serve God—but to enjoy Him.

The First Love Flame

Adoration is what keeps your first love burning. It is what returns you to the wonder of who God is. It is what keeps your spirit aligned, your prayers pure, and your heart free.

Let the first words from your lips each day be words of worship. Let your prayer life be built on the unshakable foundation of God's worthiness. Let adoration rise from your secret place and become the fragrance that marks your life. You were created to adore. Not just with your lips, but with your life. And when you do, prayer becomes not a task—but a treasure.

Activation

Choose one Psalm of praise. Read it aloud slowly, replacing "the Lord" with "You." As in speaking directly to Him. Let spontaneous words of love flow from your heart to God.

Discussion Questions

1. *Adoration fixes our eyes on who God is rather than what we need.* How does beholding God's character before presenting requests transform the atmosphere of prayer?

2. What aspects of God's nature stir your deepest awe, and how can you make adoration your first response?

3. In seasons of heaviness, how can worshipful adoration realign your emotions with eternal truth?

CHAPTER 5

THE PRAYER OF THANKSGIVING

GRATITUDE AS A WEAPON – GIVING THANKS IN ALL THINGS – SUSTAINING JOY AND PERSPECTIVE

Gratitude is more than good manners—it is a Kingdom key. It is not a polite response to blessings; it is a spiritual weapon that shifts atmospheres, disarms darkness, and aligns the soul with Heaven's perspective. The prayer of thanksgiving is not a warm-up to "real" prayer—it is one of the most powerful forms of prayer a believer can wield. It has the power to reset your mind, open your heart, and usher in God's presence.

In a world marked by entitlement, complaint, and anxiety, thanksgiving is a revolutionary act. It confronts the spirit of negativity. It breaks the chains of self-pity. It transforms the environment of the heart. The prayer of thanksgiving teaches us to praise God not just for what He has done—but for who He is, in every circumstance.

This chapter explores the deep spiritual power of gratitude. We will look at how thanksgiving is used in Scripture, why it sustains joy, how it unlocks breakthrough, and why it is a non-negotiable in every believer's prayer life. Whether you're on a mountaintop or in a valley, thanksgiving is your pathway to perspective and your entrance into presence.

1. Gratitude Is a Weapon

Thanksgiving is not just an expression—it's a weapon. It confronts the lies of the enemy, defeats the spirit of heaviness, and silences the voice of doubt. When we give thanks, we are not ignoring our problems; we are acknowledging that our God is bigger than them.

Psalm 149 says that praise binds kings with chains and nobles with fetters of iron. There is a restraining power in worship and thanksgiving that confuses and cripples demonic powers. Paul and Silas understood this when they prayed and sang hymns in prison. Their thanksgiving wasn't conditional—it was weaponized. In their darkest hour, they praised. And when they did, the prison shook and the doors flung open (Acts 16:25–26).

Many believers try to war with complaint instead of praise. But complaint empowers the enemy—thanksgiving disarms him. Complaint magnifies the problem—thanksgiving magnifies the Lord. When you begin to thank God for who He is, your spiritual posture changes. The enemy loses influence because your heart is no longer bound to fear or frustration.

Thanksgiving also confronts the spirit of pride. It acknowledges our dependence on God. Every time we give thanks, we are saying, "I didn't earn this. I didn't make this happen. God is the source, and I honor Him." Humility and thanksgiving always go together—and where humility flows, grace increases.

2. Giving Thanks in All Things

Paul's words in 1 Thessalonians 5:18 are both simple and challenging: "*Give thanks in all circumstances; for this is the will of*

God in Christ Jesus for you." Notice he does not say give thanks for all circumstances, but in them.

This is the distinguishing mark of mature believers: the ability to remain thankful in the fire, in the waiting, in the tension. Gratitude in pain is not denial—it is devotion. It declares that God is still worthy even when life is hard. It lifts the eyes above the storm and fixes them on the unshakable One.

There is a kind of thanksgiving that flows easily—when prayers are answered, doors open, provision arrives. But there is another kind of thanksgiving that flows from a deeper well. It's the kind that is chosen, not felt. It is birthed in surrender. It comes from the soul that says, "Though He slay me, yet will I trust Him" (Job 13:15).

This kind of thanksgiving is precious to God. It is worship in its purest form. It costs something. And it bears much fruit.

> *Habakkuk prayed this way in the midst of devastation:*
> *"Though the fig tree does not bud*
> *and there are no grapes on the vines,*
> *though the olive crop fails*
> *and the fields produce no food,*
> *though there are no sheep in the pen*
> *and no cattle in the stalls,*
> *yet I will rejoice in the Lord,*
> *I will be joyful in God my Savior."*
> (Habakkuk 3:17–18)

Thanksgiving in all things is not natural—it is supernatural. It flows from faith, not feeling. And the more we practice it, the more we cultivate a heart that remains steady, joyful, and rooted in truth.

3. Sustaining Joy Through Thanksgiving

Joy is not an accident. It is not the product of perfect circumstances. It is the fruit of a thankful heart. Isaiah 12:3 says, "With joy you will draw water from the wells of salvation." Joy is how we draw from God's strength. And thanksgiving is what sustains that joy.

Psalm 100 teaches us the pattern of entering God's presence: "Enter His gates with thanksgiving and His courts with praise." Thanksgiving is the gate to joy. It is the entry point to worship. Without thanksgiving, worship becomes dry. Prayer becomes mechanical. Faith becomes weak.

When we lose our gratitude, we lose our joy. And when we lose our joy, we lose our strength (Nehemiah 8:10). That's why the enemy works so hard to get you to complain, criticize, and focus on what's missing. Because if he can steal your thankfulness, he can weaken your joy and disrupt your spiritual momentum.

But the opposite is also true. When you begin to thank God —deliberately, persistently—joy begins to rise. The heaviness lifts. Perspective shifts. You start remembering His faithfulness. You start celebrating His promises. And suddenly, what felt like a burden becomes a blessing again.

Thanksgiving trains your heart to rejoice before the answer comes. It creates a spirit of contentment in the waiting. It guards your heart against bitterness and impatience. It strengthens your emotional resilience. It resets your inner climate from gloom to gladness.

4. Thanksgiving Unlocks Breakthrough

Thanksgiving doesn't just shift our perspective—it unlocks

supernatural breakthrough. Jesus demonstrated this when He fed the five thousand. He didn't begin with a request—He began with gratitude. He took the little boy's lunch, looked up to Heaven, gave thanks, and then multiplied the bread (John 6:11). Thanksgiving became the trigger for multiplication.

Again, in John 11, when Jesus stood at Lazarus's tomb, He didn't cry out in desperation. He lifted His eyes and said, "Father, I thank You that You have heard Me" (John 11:41). Then He called Lazarus forth. Resurrection followed thanksgiving. This pattern is not coincidental—it is covenantal. Thanksgiving precedes power. Praise precedes provision. God moves where gratitude creates an atmosphere of faith and expectation.

Many believers delay breakthrough because they grumble while they wait. They pray from a posture of frustration instead of faith. But when you begin to thank God before the answer comes, you demonstrate trust in His character. You release spiritual authority. And you prepare the ground for miracle manifestation.

Thanksgiving also unlocks peace. Philippians 4:6–7 gives us the formula: "Do not be anxious about anything, but in every situation, by prayer and petition, with thanksgiving, present your requests to God. And the peace of God... will guard your hearts and minds in Christ Jesus."

Peace doesn't follow prayer alone—it follows prayer seasoned with thanksgiving. If your prayers feel anxious, add gratitude. If your heart feels restless, start thanking God for every evidence of His goodness you can recall. Watch how quickly peace returns.

5. Practicing the Prayer of Thanksgiving

Thanksgiving is not just something we feel—it's something

we choose. And like every spiritual discipline, it must be practiced intentionally until it becomes instinctual. Here are a few ways to practice the prayer of thanksgiving daily:

a. Begin Every Prayer With Thanksgiving

Make it your habit to start every prayer by thanking God. Thank Him for His character, His Word, His promises, and His faithfulness in your life. This sets the tone for intimacy and lifts your heart into faith.

b. Keep a Gratitude Journal

Each day, write down three things you're thankful for. They can be big or small. Over time, this trains your mind to look for God's goodness in every situation.

c. Turn Complaints Into Praise

Every time you're tempted to complain, stop and find a reason to thank God instead. Turn "I'm tired" into "Thank You for sustaining me." Turn "I don't have enough" into "Thank You that You're my provider."

d. Memorize Thanksgiving Scriptures

Let verses like Psalm 103, 1 Chronicles 16:34, and Colossians 3:17 dwell in your spirit. Speak them out. Pray them. Let them become your default response to every situation.

e. Incorporate Thanksgiving in Corporate Prayer

When you gather with others to pray, begin with gratitude. Lead with praise. Let thanksgiving set the tone. It will stir faith and invite God's presence in a tangible way.

6. The Nature of God That Fuels Gratitude

Our thanksgiving is fueled by a continual revelation of who God is. When you know His nature, you'll never run out of reasons to thank Him. Every name of God becomes an invitation to give thanks:

- Jehovah Jireh – Thank You for being my provider.
- Jehovah Shalom – Thank You for Your peace that guards my heart.
- Jehovah Rapha – Thank You for Your healing touch over my body and soul.
- El Shaddai – Thank You that You are more than enough.
- Emmanuel – Thank You that You are always with me.

The deeper your revelation of God, the richer your gratitude will become. That's why thanksgiving and the Word must work together. The more you know of God's heart, the more your heart will overflow with praise.

7. Thanksgiving and the Spirit of Maturity

Immature believers only thank God when they feel good or when things go their way. Mature believers thank God in all things—because they've learned that He is good even when life is not. They don't just thank Him after victory—they thank Him during battle. They understand that every circumstance is an opportunity to glorify God.

Maturity in prayer is marked by consistency in thanksgiving. It is easy to ask, "Why me?" when things go wrong. It is harder—but holier—to say, "Even now, I will praise You."

The early Church modeled this kind of maturity. Persecuted,

rejected, and imprisoned, they did not grow bitter. They grew bolder. They rejoiced that they were counted worthy to suffer for Christ's name (Acts 5:41). That kind of gratitude shook nations.

Your level of thanksgiving will determine your level of joy, your clarity of vision, and your depth of trust in God. Grow in gratitude, and you will grow in spiritual authority.

Let Thanks Rise

The prayer of thanksgiving is not optional—it's essential. It is the oil that keeps the flame of devotion burning. It is the sound that shifts the atmosphere. It is the fragrance that attracts the presence of God.

Let your life become a symphony of thanksgiving. Let your secret place be filled with gratitude. Let your prayers begin and end with thanks. And watch what happens when you cultivate a heart that never ceases to give praise. For in every season, in every situation, in every valley or victory—He is worthy. And that alone is reason to give thanks.

Activation

List ten things you're thankful for today—big or small. Begin your prayer time by thanking God for each until joy rises.

Discussion Questions

1 . *Gratitude opens the gates of Heaven and guards the heart from complaint.* How does thanksgiving shift your perspective from lack to abundance in moments of pressure?

2 . What miracles in your past deserve renewed remembrance today, and how can gratitude keep them alive?

3 . How does consistent thanksgiving build spiritual resilience and invite the presence of God into everyday life?

CHAPTER 6

THE PRAYER OF CONFESSION AND REPENTANCE

CLEANSING THE HEART – RESTORING FELLOWSHIP WITH GOD – WALKING IN FREEDOM

There is no prayer more powerful to restore the heart, break the chains of guilt, and invite the presence of God than the prayer of confession and repentance. Though often neglected in modern spirituality or reduced to a quick phrase at the end of a service, confession and repentance are not relics of religious tradition—they are the divine mechanism by which the soul is cleansed, intimacy is restored, and the atmosphere is purified.

God is not seeking perfection—He is seeking honesty. And it is in the place of confession that truth meets mercy, and brokenness becomes beauty. Repentance is not punishment; it is alignment. It is the act of turning from what kills us to the One who heals us. When we pray prayers of repentance, we are not groveling—we are coming back into agreement with our original design: to walk with God in holiness and joy.

This chapter will explore why confession and repentance must be core to our prayer life, how they function biblically, what true repentance looks like, and how these prayers lead us out of shame and into freedom.

1. The Forgotten Power of Confession

To confess means to acknowledge—freely, humbly, and truthfully. In the biblical sense, it is not merely admitting wrongdoing but agreeing with God about what is wrong and why it must be dealt with. Confession says, "You are right, Lord, and I am out of alignment."

The power of confession is not in its ritual—but in its sincerity. When the heart is open, confession becomes a cleansing stream. David cried out in Psalm 32:5, "Then I acknowledged my sin to you and did not cover up my iniquity. I said, 'I will confess my transgressions to the Lord.' And You forgave the guilt of my sin."

There is both confession to God and, in certain contexts, confession to others. James 5:16 exhorts us, "Confess your sins to each other and pray for each other so that you may be healed." Confession brings things into the light. And what is exposed to light loses its power in darkness.

But many avoid confession. Why? Because pride fears exposure. Shame fears rejection. But the blood of Jesus doesn't just cover sin—it cleanses it. We don't confess to be punished—we confess to be free.

Unconfessed sin builds barriers. It silences your discernment. It dulls your hunger. It chokes your joy. But when you release it, your spirit breathes again. Fellowship is restored. Peace floods in. Worship becomes sweet again.

Confession is not just for the moment of salvation—it is a lifestyle of transparency before God.

2. Repentance: The Doorway to Transformation

If confession is the acknowledgment of sin, repentance is the decision to turn from it. It is not simply feeling bad—it is choosing change. It is not just remorse—it is a redirection of the will.

The Greek word for repentance, metanoia, literally means "a change of mind." It involves a shift in thinking that leads to a shift in behavior. True repentance is not emotional—it is intentional. Emotions may accompany it, but the fruit of repentance is not tears—it is transformation.

Jesus began His public ministry with this call: "Repent, for the Kingdom of Heaven has come near" (Matthew 4:17). In other words, "Change your thinking, because something greater has arrived." Repentance is not about shame—it's about readiness. You can't carry the Kingdom while clinging to carnality.

Paul spoke of "godly sorrow that brings repentance leading to salvation and leaves no regret" (2 Corinthians 7:10). Godly sorrow doesn't condemn—it convicts. It draws you toward God, not away from Him. It doesn't leave you hopeless—it makes you whole.

When repentance is genuine, it bears fruit. John the Baptist warned the religious crowd to "produce fruit in keeping with repentance" (Luke 3:8). This means a true turnaround is visible. It shifts how we speak, live, prioritize, and love. It doesn't just stay in the prayer closet—it walks out in daily life.

3. The Restoring Nature of God

God is not harsh when we come to Him in confession and repentance. He is a restorer. His nature is not to reject but to redeem. This is why the enemy works so hard to keep us in hiding

—because he knows the moment we return, mercy runs to meet us.

Consider the story of the prodigal son in Luke 15. The son rehearsed his confession: "Father, I have sinned against Heaven and against you." But before he could finish his speech, the father ran to him, embraced him, clothed him, and restored his identity. This is what the Father does for every returning heart.

Psalm 51 is David's prayer of repentance after his sin with Bathsheba. In it, we see the broken heart of a king who once fell but refused to stay in the dark:

> *"Have mercy on me, O God,*
> *according to Your unfailing love;*
> *according to Your great compassion*
> *blot out my transgressions.*
> *Wash away all my iniquity*
> *and cleanse me from my sin."*
> (Psalm 51:1–2)

David didn't run from God—he ran to Him. And that's why David was a man after God's heart. Not because he never sinned, but because he always returned.

God does not restore us reluctantly—He restores us joyfully. He removes the stain of sin. He silences the accuser. He revives the spirit. He reestablishes purpose. All through one humble prayer of confession and repentance.

4. Prayers That Cleanse the Heart

A heart that is consistently cleansed is a heart that remains open to God. Just as we bathe our bodies regularly, our spirits must be continually cleansed by the water of repentance. Here are a few ways to incorporate confession and repentance into your daily prayer life:

a. Ask the Holy Spirit to Search You

Psalm 139:23–24: *"Search me, O God, and know my heart... See if there is any offensive way in me."* Begin your time in prayer by inviting the Spirit to reveal anything that grieves Him. He is gentle and faithful to show you.

b. Confess Specifically

Don't hide behind vague phrases like "Forgive me for anything I've done." Be specific. Name the attitudes, words, or actions that missed the mark. Bring them into the light. When confession is specific, freedom is specific.

c. Repent with Sincerity and Faith

Turn from the sin and toward God. Declare your decision to walk in obedience. Thank Him for His cleansing. Don't wallow in guilt—receive grace with boldness.

d. Declare the Word Over Yourself

Speak verses like 1 John 1:9, Isaiah 1:18, and Psalm 103:12 aloud. Remind your soul of what God has done. Confession pulls out the poison—declaration seals in the truth.

5. Walking in Freedom, Not Condemnation

The purpose of confession and repentance is not to keep us in a cycle of shame, but to bring us into sustained freedom. Romans 8:1 declares, "There is now no condemnation for those who are in Christ Jesus."

Condemnation is the voice of the accuser. It says, "You are unworthy. You've failed too many times. You'll never change." But conviction is the voice of the Spirit. It says, "Come higher. You're made for more. Return to Me."

When we confess and repent, God doesn't just forgive us—He forgets. He casts our sin "as far as the east is from the west" (Psalm 103:12). He doesn't keep score—He cancels the record.

But walking in freedom requires that we renew our minds. After repentance, we must replace the old pattern with truth. We don't just turn from sin—we turn toward righteousness. We replace lies with Scripture. We don't just feel forgiven—we think like free people.

Freedom is not just what you're delivered from—it's what you're empowered to walk into. And it all begins in the prayer of repentance.

6. Repentance as a Lifestyle

Repentance is not just for major moral failures. It is a posture. It is the continual orientation of a heart that says, "Lord, I want to be like You. Purify me."

Isaiah was already a prophet when he saw the Lord and cried, "Woe is me, for I am undone!" (Isaiah 6:5). He wasn't in rebellion —but he was in awe. And in that holy moment, he saw his own impurity in light of God's holiness. That's repentance. And what followed was commissioning. Repentance leads to deeper intimacy and higher assignment.

Make repentance a daily rhythm—not because you're in fear, but because you desire closeness. Let the Spirit search you. Keep short accounts. Don't let pride build up. Don't let sin harden your heart. Live clean, walk free, and remain sensitive.

Return and Be Refreshed

Acts 3:19 says, *"Repent, then, and turn to God, so that your sins may be wiped out, that times of refreshing may come from the Lord."* That's the promise: Refreshing.

Repentance is not the end—it's the doorway. The doorway to revival. To refreshing. To restoration. If your heart feels dry, your passion dull, or your intimacy with God distant, the call is simple: Return.

Pray the prayer of confession. Turn in repentance. And be refreshed by the One who never grows weary of restoring His sons and daughters.

There is freedom on the other side of surrender. There is joy on the other side of confession. There is power on the other side of repentance. Let this become your prayer:

"Create in me a clean heart, O God, and renew a right spirit within me" (Psalm 51:10).

Activation

Pray Psalm 51 aloud. Pause after each verse that convicts you.
Write a personal line beginning with "Lord, create in me ..." to
capture your response.

Discussion Questions

1. *Confession exposes darkness; repentance invites renewal and intimacy.* How does honest confession restore fellowship rather than merely relieve guilt?

2. What prevents you from viewing repentance as a doorway to freedom instead of failure?

3. When was the last time repentance became worship for you, and what transformation followed?

CHAPTER 7

THE PRAYER OF PETITION AND SUPPLICATION

BRINGING YOUR REQUESTS BEFORE GOD –
PRAYING ACCORDING TO HIS WILL –
PERSISTENCE AND FAITH

P
rayer is not only the expression of worship, thanksgiving, and repentance; it is also the avenue through which we bring our needs, desires, and burdens to the throne of grace. God, as a loving Father, invites us to make requests. He is not irritated by our needs—He is moved by them. The prayer of petition and supplication is one of the most personal and powerful expressions of our dependence on God, and it reveals His desire to be our source and supply.

But not all petitions are created equal. The kind of supplication that Heaven responds to is not rooted in fear or entitlement, but in faith, reverence, and alignment with His will. In this chapter, we will explore what it means to bring your requests before God in a way that honors His Word, activates His promises, and aligns your spirit with His purposes. We will learn the difference between selfish begging and Spirit-led asking, between transactional prayer and covenant petition.

1. Petition: The Boldness to Ask

To petition means to formally present a request to a higher

authority. In prayer, it is the intentional act of bringing your needs before God—asking Him to intervene, provide, protect, or act on your behalf. Petition is not casual; it is purposeful. It is the posture of a son or daughter who understands both the generosity of the Father and the access they've been granted through Christ.

Hebrews 4:16 says, "*Let us then approach God's throne of grace with confidence, so that we may receive mercy and find grace to help us in our time of need.*" This invitation is remarkable. We are not told to come timidly, fearfully, or reluctantly—but boldly. Why? Because Jesus, our High Priest, has already made a way.

There is nothing weak about asking God to move in your life. Jesus Himself said, "Ask and it will be given to you; seek and you will find; knock and the door will be opened to you" (Matthew 7:7). The tense in Greek implies continual action: keep asking, keep seeking, keep knocking. Petition is not a one-time plea—it is the persistent pursuit of Heaven's response.

Asking reveals relationship. Children don't hesitate to ask their parents for what they need. Why? Because they know they are loved, covered, and heard. We must recover this childlike faith in our petitions—not a faith that demands, but a faith that trusts the Father's goodness.

2. Supplication: The Depth of Desperation

Supplication is closely related to petition, but it carries a deeper sense of humility and urgency. While petition emphasizes access, supplication emphasizes posture. It is the kind of prayer that flows from a heart fully surrendered, fully dependent, and fully aware of its need for God.

Paul uses this language in Philippians 4:6: "Do not be anxious about anything, but in everything by prayer and supplication with thanksgiving let your requests be made known to God." Supplication is not whining or emotionalism—it is fervent, focused, and Spirit-filled pleading that touches the heart of God.

Jesus demonstrated this in the garden of Gethsemane. Luke 22:44 says, "Being in anguish, He prayed more earnestly, and His sweat was like drops of blood falling to the ground." This was not casual prayer. It was supplication. It was the kind of prayer that presses beyond comfort into the place of surrender.

Supplication does not manipulate God—it moves Him because it is honest, raw, and reverent. It is the cry of Hannah in the temple, groaning for a son. It is the desperation of blind Bartimaeus shouting, "Jesus, Son of David, have mercy on me!" It is the posture of the persistent widow, who would not stop until justice was given.

3. Praying According to His Will

One of the most important aspects of effective petition and supplication is alignment. God is not a genie; He is a King. His throne is not a place of wish fulfillment—it is a place of holy partnership. And for our prayers to be powerful, they must align with His will.

1 John 5:14–15 says, "This is the confidence we have in approaching God: that if we ask anything according to His will, He hears us. And if we know that He hears us—whatever we ask—we know that we have what we asked of Him." The secret to answered prayer is not volume—it's alignment. How do we know His will? Through His Word and His Spirit.

The Bible reveals the will of God in principle. The Holy Spirit reveals the will of God in practice. Together, they guide our petitions. For example, healing, provision, salvation, deliverance—

these are all clearly within the revealed will of God. But specifics —who to marry, what job to take, when to move—require sensitivity to the Spirit.

When your heart is surrendered and your mind renewed by Scripture, your petitions shift from self-centered to Kingdom-centered. You begin to pray not just for comfort, but for calling. Not just for success, but for sanctification. Not just for breakthrough, but for purpose.

And here's the paradox: when you seek His will first, you often receive more than you imagined. God is not stingy. He is extravagant. But He only trusts abundance to those who have learned to pray according to His will.

4. Persistence in Petition

Jesus told a parable in Luke 18 about a widow who kept coming to a corrupt judge until he gave her justice, simply to get her to stop bothering him. Then Jesus said, "Will not God bring about justice for His chosen ones, who cry out to Him day and night?" (v. 7).

Persistence in prayer is not about convincing God—it's about forming you. Something happens in the waiting. In the asking. In the returning again and again. Your faith deepens. Your priorities realign. Your desperation matures.

Too many give up after one unanswered prayer. But in the Kingdom, delay is not denial. Persistence is a sign of faith, not of doubt. Elijah prayed seven times for the rain to fall—even after the word of the Lord had been spoken. Daniel fasted and prayed for 21 days before the angel broke through. Jesus told us to "always pray and not give up." Why? Because persistence demonstrates hunger. And hunger always moves Heaven.

When you are praying according to God's will, don't stop. Don't back down. Keep knocking. Keep believing. Keep presenting your petition until the cloud forms, the door opens, the healing manifests, the prodigal returns.

5. Praying With Faith and Confidence

Faith is the currency of Heaven. Without it, it is impossible to please God (Hebrews 11:6). But with it, we move mountains, silence fear, and obtain promises. The prayer of petition must be saturated in faith—not hype or emotionalism, but confident trust in God's character.

Mark 11:24 says, "Therefore I tell you, whatever you ask for in prayer, believe that you have received it, and it will be yours." Jesus was not promoting a name-it-and-claim-it theology. He was teaching the principle of expectation. True faith prays from the answer, not just for the answer.

This means your language matters. Don't just pray problem-focused prayers—pray promise-centered ones. Instead of, "God, I don't know if You'll ever provide," say, "Father, I thank You that You are Jehovah Jireh. You know my need, and You are faithful to supply."

Faith is not wishful thinking—it is anchored assurance. It doesn't deny reality—it places trust in a greater reality. When you pray with faith, you stop begging and start declaring. You stop doubting and start rejoicing.

6. Common Pitfalls in Petition

Even with the best intentions, there are pitfalls that can hinder your prayers:

- Praying outside of God's will: Asking for things that feed the flesh instead of fulfilling God's purpose.
- Lack of faith or expectation: Praying out of obligation, not trust.
- Unforgiveness or hidden sin: These can block the flow of answered prayer (Psalm 66:18; Mark 11:25).
- Self-centeredness: James 4:3 says, "You ask and do not receive, because you ask with wrong motives..."

Avoiding these pitfalls requires a heart that is surrendered, a mind that is renewed, and a spirit that is attuned to God's voice.

7. How to Pray Petition and Supplication Effectively

Here's a practical framework for how to bring your requests before God:

a. Begin with Worship and Thanksgiving

Always enter with praise. It re-centers your soul and aligns you with God's character.

b. Present Your Request Clearly

Be specific. Name your need. Jesus often asked, "What do you want Me to do for you?" Don't be vague—be precise.

c. Anchor It in Scripture

Find promises that align with your request. Declare them. Stand on them.

d. Submit to His Will

Even Jesus prayed, "Not My will, but Yours be done." Ask boldly, but trust deeply.

e. Ask With Faith

Believe that He hears you. Expect answers. Pray from a posture of confidence.

f. Remain in Persistence

Don't stop until the answer comes or peace settles in your spirit.

The God Who Answers

The prayer of petition and supplication is not a lesser form of prayer—it is an act of bold trust, holy desperation, and covenant confidence. You are not a beggar outside the gate—you are a son or daughter standing in the throne room. You have access. You have favor. You have the right to ask.

Bring your needs before the Lord. Cry out with reverence. Ask in faith. Persist with endurance. Align with His will. And watch as Heaven responds.

He is still the God who says: *"Call to Me, and I will answer you and tell you great and unsearchable things you do not know"* (Jeremiah 33:3).

Activation

Write three petitions that reflect faith, not anxiety. Present them before God, then spend a few minutes thanking Him for hearing.

Discussion Questions

1. *Petition is the humble expression of dependence; faith turns requests into declarations of trust.* How can you present needs boldly without drifting into entitlement or anxiety?

2. What difference do you see between praying *from* lack and praying *from* inheritance?

3. How might unanswered petitions invite deeper intimacy rather than disappointment?

CHAPTER 8

THE PRAYER OF INTERCESSION

STANDING IN THE GAP – BURDEN-BEARING AND WARFARE – BIBLICAL EXAMPLES (ABRAHAM, MOSES, JESUS)

The prayer of intercession is one of the highest and most selfless forms of prayer. It is the act of stepping between Heaven and earth, standing in the gap between God's justice and man's need, and partnering with His heart to see His will established in the lives of others. Intercession is where compassion becomes action. It is where the heart of God is carried by His sons and daughters who are willing to weep where He weeps, war where He wars, and believe where others have lost hope.

To intercede is to intercept. It means to interrupt the enemy's agenda and call forth the purposes of God. Intercessors are watchmen, warriors, and burden-bearers. They are not content to sit idly by while destruction, deception, or delay ravages people and places. They rise, they cry out, they war, and they contend.

In this chapter, we will dive deep into the calling, cost, and reward of the prayer of intercession. We will study the lives of biblical intercessors, unpack what it means to carry a burden in the Spirit, and explore how intercession shapes history, shifts atmospheres, and releases the will of God into the earth.

1. What Is Intercession?

Intercession means to plead, mediate, or intervene on behalf of another. It is not merely praying for someone—it is standing in the place of someone. It is identification prayer, where the intercessor lays hold of God and refuses to let go until the mercy, power, or deliverance of God is released into that situation.

The Hebrew word paga used for intercession means "to meet," "to encounter," or "to strike." Intercession is a collision point between the kingdom of darkness and the Kingdom of God. It's where spiritual resistance is confronted by spiritual authority.

Isaiah 59:16 says, *"He saw that there was no one, He was appalled that there was no one to intervene."* God seeks those who will intervene—those who will not just pray for their own lives, but will stand for others when they cannot stand for themselves.

Intercession is not passive. It is priestly and prophetic. It's priestly because it lifts up others before God, and it's prophetic because it declares and enforces Heaven's agenda over their lives.

2. The Burden of the Lord: Carrying His Heart

Intercession begins with burden. Not emotional burden, but spiritual burden—weight from God's heart placed upon yours. True intercessors do not choose their assignments. They are entrusted with them. They don't just pray from knowledge; they pray from divine compassion.

Jeremiah said, *"My anguish, my anguish! I writhe in pain... I cannot keep silent, for I have heard the sound of the trumpet; I have heard the battle cry"* (Jeremiah 4:19). That is what intercession feels like. A cry that erupts from the spirit. A fire that burns within. A groan too deep for words.

Romans 8:26–27 tells us that the Holy Spirit Himself intercedes through us with groanings that cannot be uttered. When you become an intercessor, you become a vessel for the burden of the Lord. He entrusts you with secrets, tears, and cries that mirror His own.

This burden can come suddenly or grow over time. It can last for a moment, a season, or a lifetime. But it always produces prayer. Deep, fervent, focused prayer that breaks chains, births destiny, and rebuilds broken places.

3. Standing in the Gap: Abraham and Moses

The phrase "standing in the gap" comes from Ezekiel 22:30, where God says, "*I looked for someone among them who would build up the wall and stand before Me in the gap on behalf of the land so I would not destroy it, but I found no one.*"

To stand in the gap means to position yourself between judgment and mercy, pleading with God for intervention. It is the posture of Abraham, who interceded for Sodom, saying, "Will You destroy the righteous with the wicked? Suppose there are fifty righteous..." (Genesis 18). Abraham was not just concerned for his nephew Lot—he was contending for a city. He appealed to God's justice and mercy, negotiating in prayer with holy reverence.

Moses also stood in the gap. When Israel worshipped the golden calf and provoked God's wrath, Moses cried out, "But now, please forgive their sin—but if not, blot me out of the book You have written" (Exodus 32:32). That is the heart of an intercessor: willing to bear the cost for the sake of others.

God responded to both men because their intercession flowed from relationship. They knew God. They carried His heart. They spoke as friends, not strangers. Their words were not rehearsed—they were weighty. Their prayers weren't polished—they were powerful.

4. Jesus the Intercessor

The greatest intercessor in history is Jesus Himself. Hebrews 7:25 says, *"He ever lives to make intercession for them."* Even now, seated at the right hand of the Father, Jesus is interceding for us. His intercession didn't stop at the cross—it continues in eternity.

On earth, Jesus modeled intercession. In John 17, we find His high priestly prayer, where He prays not only for His disciples, but for all who would believe through their message. He prays for unity, sanctification, and the revelation of glory. This is intercession at its highest—praying from the heart of the Father for the destiny of generations.

On the cross, Jesus interceded for His enemies: "Father, forgive them, for they know not what they do" (Luke 23:34). He bore our sin, our curse, our punishment—so that we could be reconciled. His blood speaks better things than Abel's. It cries out not for vengeance, but for mercy.

To be an intercessor is to become like Jesus. To bear the burdens of others, to cry out for their deliverance, to groan for their salvation, to plead for their restoration.

5. The Cost of Intercession

Intercession is costly. It demands time, focus, humility, and sometimes tears. It requires that you shift from self-centered prayers to Kingdom-centered warfare. Intercessors are often misunderstood, unseen, and spiritually attacked—because the enemy fears those who know how to stand in the spirit. The cost includes:

- Emotional investment: You feel what others cannot feel. You carry what others ignore.
- Spiritual warfare: Intercession brings you into direct conflict with principalities and powers.
- Time and inconvenience: Burdens may come in the night. You may be called to weep, fast, or war at unexpected moments.
- Rejection and loneliness: Like watchmen on the wall, intercessors are often ahead of what others see and hear.

But the reward is eternal. Souls are saved. Nations are shifted. Marriages are restored. Churches are revived. Demonic strongholds are torn down. And the intercessor, though unseen on earth, is honored in Heaven.

6. Intercession as Warfare

Intercession is not just compassion—it is confrontation. It confronts the enemy's plans with Heaven's purposes. When you intercede, you step into the gap between what is and what God says should be. You battle in the spirit for the fulfillment of God's Word.

Paul exhorted Timothy to "wage the good warfare by the prophecies previously made concerning you" (1 Timothy 1:18). This is intercessory warfare—praying into fulfillment what God has spoken. You don't accept delay, you war until manifestation.

Intercession binds and looses. It binds demonic activity and looses divine intervention. It breaks curses and enforces covenant. It partners with angels and paralyzes hell.

It is often accompanied by fasting, groaning, travail, and prophetic insight. It is not a gentle prayer—it is a violent love. Intercession is what delivers drug addicts, shakes cities, births revivals, and resurrects dead things.

7. Practical Ways to Grow in Intercession

If you feel the call to intercede, here are practical steps to grow:

a. Spend Time Listening

Let God share His burdens with you. Ask Him, "What's on Your heart today?" Write it down.

b. Study the Word

Let Scripture guide your intercession. Pray promises, not just problems.

c. Build a Watch List

Keep a list of people, places, or causes God has placed on your heart. Pray over them consistently.

d. Join or Lead a Prayer Group

Intercession multiplies in community. Gather with others who carry the burden of prayer.

e. Fast Regularly

Fasting sharpens discernment and increases spiritual authority in intercession.

f. Record Breakthroughs

Track the answers to your intercession. It will build faith and remind you that your labor is not in vain.

Becoming God's Watchman

The Lord is still searching for intercessors. For those who will stand in the gap and refuse to let go. For those who will carry the burdens of others and cry out until breakthrough comes. For those who will weep between the porch and the altar and release revival into dry places.

You were not saved to sit on the sidelines. You were born again to stand in the spirit and war for those who cannot yet war for themselves. You were called to be a watchman. A priest. A gap-filler. A Kingdom enforcer.

Rise, intercessor. The hour is urgent. The battle is real. But Heaven is backing you. And Jesus is praying with you.

Activation

*Ask the Spirit for one person or issue to intercede over this week. Pray
daily for them, journaling any insight or burden you sense.*

Discussion Questions

1. *Intercession stands in the gap so others can encounter mercy
instead of judgment.* What does it mean to carry another's
burden before God without becoming crushed by it?

2. How can compassion mature into authority in your
intercession for people or nations?

3. Recall a time intercession shifted an atmosphere—what
spiritual principles were at work?

CHAPTER 9

THE PRAYER OF AGREEMENT

THE POWER OF UNITY IN PRAYER – PRAYING WITH OTHERS EFFECTIVELY – PRAYER PARTNERS AND CORPORATE PRAYER

There are few forces more powerful on the earth than two believers who are in agreement with Heaven and one another. The prayer of agreement is not merely simultaneous prayer—it is spiritual synergy. It is what happens when hearts, voices, and faith are joined together under the authority of God's Word and the leading of the Holy Spirit to see His will manifest in the earth.

We were never meant to carry the burden of prayer alone. From the earliest pages of Scripture, we see that God blesses unity, multiplies faith, and honors agreement. The power of one intercessor is great, but the power of agreement is exponential. Where isolated faith may shake a room, united faith can shake a city.

In this chapter, we will examine the biblical basis for the prayer of agreement, explore the dynamics of corporate prayer, understand how to cultivate prayer partnerships, and unlock the supernatural realm that agreement in the Spirit releases.

1. The Authority of Agreement

Jesus taught plainly in Matthew 18:19–20:

"Again I say to you, that if two of you agree on earth concerning anything that they ask, it will be done for them by My Father in Heaven. For where two or three are gathered together in My name, I am there in the midst of them."

This is not poetic encouragement—it is legal authority. The word "agree" in the Greek is sumphoneo, where we get the word "symphony." It means to sound together, to be in harmonious alignment. The prayer of agreement is not simply saying the same thing at the same time; it is unity of spirit, mind, and voice.

Heaven recognizes unity. Agreement multiplies authority. One can put a thousand to flight, but two can put ten thousand (Deuteronomy 32:30). That's not addition—it's multiplication. When believers come into true agreement, something is released in the spirit realm that cannot be accomplished alone.

This principle is rooted in the very nature of God, who exists in eternal unity—Father, Son, and Holy Spirit. All true agreement flows from divine order and relational honor.

2. The Blueprint of Early Church Agreement

The book of Acts gives us a powerful model of the prayer of agreement in action. Before Pentecost, we find the 120 in the upper room, "with one accord in prayer and supplication" (Acts 1:14). That phrase "one accord" speaks of unanimous focus, unified pursuit, and spiritual harmony.

When the day of Pentecost fully came, they were still in "one place and one accord" (Acts 2:1). The fire fell not simply because they were present—but because they were united. The prayer of agreement created a habitation for the Holy Spirit.

Again in Acts 4, when the apostles were threatened and released, they returned to their own people and "raised their voices together in prayer to God" (Acts 4:24). As they agreed in prayer, the place was shaken, and they were filled with boldness and power.

Agreement in prayer releases supernatural response. God not only hears—it moves Him. He attends to unity with fire, boldness, healing, and open doors.

3. Hindrances to Agreement

True agreement cannot be forced or faked. It is not simply praying next to someone—it is being aligned with them in spirit, faith, and intent. There are several hindrances that can undermine the power of agreement:

a. Unforgiveness or Offense

Jesus taught in the same passage about agreement that we must forgive our brother (Matthew 18:21–22). Bitterness breaks agreement. If there is relational tension, prayer becomes limited (1 Peter 3:7).

b. Misalignment in Purpose

Agreement cannot exist when there are competing agendas. If one is praying for personal gain and the other for Kingdom advancement, the synergy is broken.

c. Lack of Honor

Spiritual authority flows through honor. Where there is dishonor—whether of leaders, spouses, or one another—the unity necessary for breakthrough cannot be sustained.

d. Presumption Without Submission

You cannot claim Matthew 18:19 without first walking in Matthew 18:15–18, which outlines accountability, submission, and relational order. Agreement is born in the soil of healthy relationships.

4. Cultivating Effective Prayer Partnerships

Not every believer is called to walk with everyone at the same level of spiritual agreement. Just as Jesus had crowds, a core twelve, and an inner circle of three, we too must discern who we walk closely with in prayer.

An effective prayer partner is not just someone who prays—they are someone who is mature, submitted, Spirit-led, and aligned in faith and purpose. They don't just agree with your desires—they agree with Heaven's will. Here are qualities to look for in a prayer partner:

- They carry a lifestyle of consecration and holiness.
- They are willing to pray consistently and fervently.
- They are not intimidated by warfare or waiting.
- They are sensitive to the Holy Spirit.
- They speak life and truth, not doubt or flattery.
- They listen to God, not just talk to Him.

When you find such a partner, treat that relationship as a gift. Guard it with integrity, humility, and intentionality.

5. The Dynamics of Corporate Prayer

Corporate prayer is the expansion of agreement from two or

three to a gathered assembly of believers. Throughout Scripture, God moved mightily when His people prayed in unity.

In Joel 2, the priests and people gathered, wept, and fasted—and God promised to pour out His Spirit. In 2 Chronicles 20, Jehoshaphat called all Judah to seek the Lord. As they worshipped in unity, the Lord set ambushes against their enemies. There are several dynamics to understand in corporate prayer:

a. Unity of Focus

Corporate prayer should have a clear objective. Wandering prayers create confusion. Unified prayer creates power.

b. Alignment with Leadership

When the leadership of a house sets the focus, the people align. Corporate prayer is not a free-for-all; it's a coordinated battle plan.

c. Room for Expression, Honor for Order

While liberty in the Spirit is vital, honoring the flow and authority of the moment is equally vital. One rogue voice can derail a corporate moment.

d. Declaration Over Discussion

Corporate prayer is not a brainstorming session. It is a time to declare, intercede, and war—not to talk about problems endlessly.

6. The Prophetic Power of Agreement

The prayer of agreement doesn't just respond to needs—it

enforces prophecy. When believers agree over a promise, they partner with Heaven to call that word into manifestation.

Paul told Timothy to wage warfare with the prophecies made about him (1 Timothy 1:18). When you and another believer agree over what God has spoken, you create a courtroom witness. You are saying, "Let it be established on earth as it is in Heaven."

This kind of agreement carries apostolic power. It establishes boundaries in the Spirit. It tears down strongholds. It releases angels. It births movements. It opens cities.

When prophetic voices gather in unity—declaring the same word, in the same spirit, under the same covering—the enemy trembles. Agreement is not soft—it is thunderous.

7. Agreement in Marriage

Perhaps one of the most underestimated dimensions of the prayer of agreement is in marriage. Scripture is clear: "*If two of you agree...*" (Matthew 18:19). Who better than husband and wife?

1 Peter 3:7 warns that if husbands are not treating their wives with honor, their prayers will be hindered. This shows the seriousness of relational unity in prayer. Marriages that pray together tap into a level of divine agreement that multiplies breakthrough. Married couples should:

- Set regular times to pray together.
- Agree on prayer points for family, finances, and ministry.
- Forgive quickly and refuse to let offense linger.
- Speak blessing and identity over one another.
- Intercede for each other's dreams and assignments.

Hell fears a married couple in agreement. Because their unity is not just emotional—it's spiritual.

8. When Agreement Unlocks Revival

Every major revival in history was preceded by united prayer. The Moravians, the Welsh Revival, Azusa Street, and others all began when a remnant agreed in prayer for Heaven to invade earth.

Revival does not fall randomly. It falls on the altar of unity. When leaders, intercessors, and churches begin to cry out with one heart and one voice, Heaven responds.

We must move from isolated intercession to corporate agreement. From personal breakthroughs to regional awakenings. When agreement becomes a culture in prayer rooms, churches, and cities, strongholds begin to break and the atmosphere begins to shift.

Let the Sound of Agreement Rise

The sound of agreement is not soft. It is not passive. It is not hesitant. It is bold, unified, and faith-filled. It is the sound of one heart, one voice, and one Spirit crying out for the will of God to be done on earth as it is in Heaven.

When you find those who will agree with you in prayer, you have found treasure. Steward it well. When you enter a room filled with unified intercessors, you have entered a gate of Heaven. Walk in reverence. Release your voice. Stand in faith.

Let the prayer of agreement rise in homes, churches, and cities. Let leaders humble themselves and unite. Let prayer partners be raised up and sustained. Let corporate gatherings become divine councils where Heaven's will is sealed through agreement. Because when two or three gather in His name—and agree—anything becomes possible.

Activation

Invite a trusted believer to agree with you on one promise of God. Together declare that promise aloud for seven consecutive days.

Discussion Questions

1. *Agreement unites believers under Heaven's will, multiplying authority through unity.* Why does spiritual agreement require purity of motive as much as similarity of request?

2. How can you discern when unity is genuine partnership versus pressured conformity?

3. What would change in your community if believers truly agreed around God's Word rather than opinion?

CHAPTER 10

THE PRAYER OF DECLARATION AND DECREE

SPEAKING GOD'S WORD WITH AUTHORITY – ALIGNING WITH HEAVEN'S VERDICT – CREATING SHIFTS THROUGH SPOKEN PRAYER

There are times in prayer when we ask. There are times when we intercede. There are times when we listen. And there are times when we speak—boldly, prophetically, and with Heaven's authority. This is the prayer of declaration and decree.

Declaration is not hopeful wishing—it is authoritative speaking. Decree is not casual language—it is governmental enforcement. When we declare and decree in prayer, we are not trying to convince God or inform Him—we are aligning ourselves with His already-settled Word and releasing that truth into the atmosphere to overthrow lies, break demonic power, and call things into order.

The Kingdom of God is voice-activated. Creation began with, "Let there be..." not with silence or hesitation. From Genesis to Revelation, the pattern is clear: God speaks, His people echo, and the world shifts. In this chapter, we'll explore the difference between declarations and decrees, understand the biblical foundation for speaking with authority, and learn how our words, filled with God's Spirit and rooted in His Word, become weapons of war and instruments of dominion.

1. The Power of the Spoken Word

Proverbs 18:21 declares, *"Death and life are in the power of the tongue, and those who love it will eat its fruit."* That's not metaphor—it's spiritual reality. Words are not empty. In the Kingdom, they are containers of power.

Hebrews 11:3 tells us that the worlds were framed by the Word of God. God did not create silently—He created by speaking. *"Let there be light..."* And there was. When we speak God's Word, we are not simply reciting—we are framing spiritual realities, releasing truth into darkness, and setting boundaries where chaos once ruled.

Jesus said in Mark 11:23, *"Whoever says to this mountain, 'Be removed and be cast into the sea,' and does not doubt in his heart... he will have whatever he says."* The mountain doesn't move because you thought about it. It moves because you spoke to it in faith.

This is the foundation of declaration and decree. It is not shouting to sound spiritual. It is commanding to establish order. It is not arrogance—it is alignment. You are not inventing power —you are exercising delegated authority.

2. Declaration vs. Decree: What's the Difference?

These two terms are often used interchangeably, but they carry unique nuances in Scripture and practice.

Declaration

To declare means to announce, proclaim, or boldly speak what is true. In prayer, declarations are faith-filled confessions of God's promises, nature, and intent. You declare what Heaven says is already real. Examples:

- "I declare that no weapon formed against me will prosper."
- "I declare that I am the righteousness of God in Christ."
- "I declare healing, restoration, and breakthrough in my home."

Declarations release identity, shift perspective, and awaken faith. They are not suggestions—they are proclamations rooted in the Word.

Decree

To decree is to issue a formal and binding command, backed by legal or governmental authority. In the biblical sense, decrees are verdicts aligned with the King's will, spoken by those who carry His authority on the earth.

Job 22:28 says, "You shall also decree a thing, and it shall be established for you; so light will shine on your ways." Decrees don't just proclaim—they establish. They create legal change in the spirit realm. They challenge opposing forces and enforce Kingdom rule. Examples:

- "I decree that every assignment of the enemy against my family is canceled."
- "I decree that the gates of this city are open to the Gospel."
- "I decree that this territory belongs to the Lord and no unclean spirit shall remain."

Declarations affirm truth. Decrees enforce it.

3. The Legal Authority of the Believer

You cannot decree effectively if you do not know who you are. Authority in prayer flows from identity in Christ. You are not a beggar hoping for favor—you are a citizen of Heaven and ambassador of the King.

Jesus said in Luke 10:19, *"Behold, I give you the authority... over all the power of the enemy, and nothing shall by any means hurt you."* Authority is not based on your feelings—it's based on your position.

We are seated with Christ in heavenly places (Ephesians 2:6). That is not poetic—it is jurisdictional. When you pray from this seat, you're not under attack—you're above it. You're not pleading for survival—you're enforcing victory.

Declarations and decrees are the legal language of spiritual government. Like a judge in a courtroom, you are not arguing— you are issuing verdicts. You are declaring what has already been ruled in Heaven. When your words match His Word, angels move, darkness trembles, and atmospheres shift.

4. Jesus as the Model of Decreeing Prayer

Jesus never begged demons to leave. He never negotiated with storms. He never timidly asked for healing. He declared. He decreed. He spoke as one who carried governmental authority.

- He said to the storm, "Peace, be still." And it obeyed (Mark 4:39).
- He said to the leper, "Be cleansed." And he was (Matthew 8:3).

- He said to the dead girl, "Little girl, arise." And she did (Mark 5:41).

Jesus taught us that effective prayer is not always about long words—it's about spiritual authority. When He said, "Speak to the mountain," He was inviting us into His model. Declaration and decree is not hype or emotionalism—it is spiritual governance. Jesus ruled by speaking. So do we.

5. When to Declare and Decree

Not every prayer is a decree. Discernment is required. You must know when to weep, when to wait, when to intercede—and when to stand in authority and speak. Here are moments to declare and decree:

a. When Facing Opposition

When resistance rises against God's Word over your life, decree the opposite. Speak God's promises over every lie and bind every opposing spirit.

b. When Releasing Prophetic Words

When a prophetic word aligns with Scripture and has been confirmed, decree it into the atmosphere. Decrees seal what has been spoken and invite manifestation.

c. When Warring for Territory

Declare God's ownership over homes, cities, churches, and regions. Decree His reign over darkness. Walk the land and speak the Word with boldness.

d. When Speaking Identity

Use declarations to anchor yourself and others in their God-given identity. Declare who you are in Christ until the soul aligns with the Spirit.

6. How to Declare and Decree Effectively

Declarations and decrees must be intentional, scriptural, and Spirit-led. Here's how to do it well:

a. Know the Word

You cannot decree what you don't know. Fill your heart with Scripture. God only backs what He has said. Your declarations must be aligned with His truth.

b. Believe What You Say

Faith is the fuel of declarations. Speak with conviction. Don't recite—release. Your words carry power when they are spoken from the place of belief.

c. Speak with Authority, Not Arrogance

Authority doesn't shout—it stands. You don't need to be loud to be powerful, but you do need to be confident. Authority flows from alignment, not volume.

d. Be Consistent

Declarations are not one-time events. Speak them daily. Speak them until your atmosphere changes, until your heart believes it, and until your situation bends to Heaven's will.

7. Examples of Declarations and Decrees

Let these examples stir your faith:

- "I declare that I am seated with Christ in Heavenly places and no weapon formed against me shall prosper."
- "I decree that my home is a dwelling place for the presence of God."
- "I declare that the joy of the Lord is my strength and depression cannot stay."
- "I decree that this ministry will walk in financial overflow and Kingdom impact."
- "I declare that I have the mind of Christ, and confusion must go."
- "I decree that revival is coming to my city, and no stronghold will stand against it."

8. Prophetic Decrees and Apostolic Authority

In apostolic and prophetic ministry, declarations and decrees become even more strategic. Prophetic decrees don't just respond —they create. Apostolic decrees don't just protect—they advance.

When prophets and apostles operate in alignment, they establish divine infrastructure. They speak Heaven's blueprint into earth's chaos. They call order to disorder, light to darkness, and future to present.

In this dimension, decrees are not reactive—they're governmental. They are spoken over cities, regions, nations, and generations. They are not casual—they are covenantal. And they must be carried with weight, holiness, and humility.

Let the King's Word Be in Your Mouth

You are not powerless. You are not voiceless. You are not a victim of the times—you are an agent of the Kingdom. Your words matter. Your voice carries weight. And when you declare and decree in alignment with God's will, nothing can stand against it.

Let your tongue become a sword. Let your declarations shake the gates of hell. Let your decrees frame the future. And let the Word of the King be in your mouth. Because in the Kingdom, what you say in faith—He will establish in power.

Activation

Choose three verses that express God's will for your situation. Speak them aloud daily, believing your words align Heaven and earth.

Discussion Questions

1 . *Declarations enforce Heaven's verdicts; decrees release divine authority on Earth.* How do you distinguish between presumption and prophetic decree when speaking God's Word?

2 . What truths from Scripture are you called to declare until reality aligns with promise?

3 . How does understanding your identity as an heir influence the confidence of your declarations?

CHAPTER 11

THE PRAYER OF LISTENING AND WAITING

THE ART OF STILLNESS – HEARING GOD'S VOICE – DISCERNING DIRECTION

In a world of noise, the discipline of stillness is radical. In a generation trained to speak, post, and perform, the ability to listen is rare. Yet in the Kingdom of God, silence is not absence—it's access. God is a speaking God. He is not silent; He is strategic. But He often waits until we are quiet enough to hear Him.

Too often, prayer has been reduced to a monologue—us speaking at God rather than communing with Him. But prayer was never meant to be one-sided. God desires dialogue. He invites us to speak—but also to wait, to listen, and to receive.

The prayer of listening and waiting is not about inactivity—it is about intentional stillness. It's not laziness—it's trust. It is the mature posture of those who know that hearing God's voice is more valuable than simply airing their opinions. In this chapter, we will journey into the art of waiting, the practice of listening, and the reward of receiving divine direction in the secret place.

1. The Lost Discipline of Stillness

Psalm 46:10 gives a divine command that serves as a foundation for this form of prayer: *"Be still, and know that I am God."* This is more than a poetic line. It is a blueprint for encounter. The word "still" in Hebrew (raphah) means to let go, to cease striving, to surrender.

Stillness is not passivity—it is positioning. It is the act of slowing our mind, emotions, and spirit long enough to allow God's presence to become central again. In the busyness of life and ministry, we can become so consumed with doing for God that we forget how to simply be with God.

Listening prayer requires stillness not just externally but internally. It is possible to sit silently while your mind is racing, your emotions are storming, and your spirit is disconnected. True listening comes when the soul quiets down and the spirit rises up.

2. Jesus Modeled the Listening Life

Jesus was not just a teacher of prayer—He was a practitioner of intimacy. His ministry was not driven by public demand but guided by private revelation. Luke 5:16 tells us, *"But Jesus often withdrew to lonely places and prayed."* He didn't pray to perform —He prayed to hear.

John 5:19 gives us a powerful glimpse into His inner world: *"The Son can do nothing by Himself; He can do only what He sees His Father doing..."* Jesus didn't react—He responded to what He heard and saw in the presence of the Father. His clarity came not from His gifting but from His devotion to stillness.

Jesus listened before He spoke. He waited before He moved. He discerned the Father's will before He acted. This is not weakness—it is wisdom. And it is a model for us to follow.

3. Hearing God's Voice

Many believers struggle with listening prayer because they doubt whether they can truly hear God. But Scripture is clear: "*My sheep hear My voice*" (John 10:27). Hearing God is not for the elite—it is the inheritance of every child of God. God speaks in many ways:

- Through His Word
- By His Spirit in our hearts
- Through visions and dreams
- By divine impressions
- Through godly counsel
- In the still, small voice (1 Kings 19:12)

The key is not whether God is speaking—the key is whether we've been trained to listen. Like Samuel in the tabernacle, we must learn the difference between religious noise and the whisper of the Lord (1 Samuel 3). The boy who ministered in routine became the prophet who heard when he said, "Speak, Lord, for Your servant is listening."

4. The Posture of Waiting

Isaiah 40:31 declares, "But those who wait on the Lord shall renew their strength..." Waiting is not wasted time—it is transformative time. It is in the waiting that strength is exchanged, that clarity is received, and that direction is discerned.

In Hebrew, the word for wait (qavah) means to bind together through twisting, like cords being braided. Waiting on the Lord is not sitting bored—it is becoming entwined with His heart. It is letting His Spirit braid your soul into His will.

There are several postures of waiting:

a. Waiting in Worship

This is not singing to fill time—it's honoring His presence without rushing Him. Worshipful waiting silences distraction and magnifies awareness.

b. Waiting in Silence

Turn off the music. Close the journal. Stop rehearsing your prayer list. Just be still. This trains your inner ear to hear beyond the noise.

c. Waiting in the Word

Meditate slowly on Scripture, asking God to highlight what He is saying. His voice is always consistent with His written Word.

d. Waiting in Surrender

Release your expectations, timelines, and agendas. Waiting is the altar where control dies and trust is reborn.

5. Discerning Divine Direction

Listening and waiting are not just for intimacy—they are also for instruction. God longs to guide His people. Psalm 32:8 promises, *"I will instruct you and teach you in the way you should go; I will guide you with My eye."*

When you quiet yourself before the Lord, you position yourself to receive strategy. He may give you a prompting, a word of wisdom, a phrase, or a mental picture. Sometimes He says much —other times He says little. But even His silence is formative. It cultivates humility, faith, and patience.

Discernment is sharpened in the secret place. The more you listen, the more familiar His voice becomes. You begin to discern the difference between the voice of your soul, the voice of the enemy, and the voice of your Shepherd.

Don't rush direction. The Lord is not in a hurry. Trust that what you need to know, He will reveal in His perfect timing. Your job is not to force answers—it is to remain present, surrendered, and attentive.

6. Obstacles to Listening and Waiting

Why do so few believers truly walk in this form of prayer? Because it is costly. It requires more than time—it requires surrender. Here are a few common hindrances:

a. Impatience

In a culture of instant gratification, waiting feels like weakness. But Kingdom maturity is marked by those who know how to linger.

b. Inner Clutter

An anxious mind, distracted soul, or overloaded schedule will drown out the whisper of the Spirit. You must declutter to hear.

c. Fear of Silence

Some avoid listening prayer because they fear God won't speak. But faith says, "Even if He is quiet, I trust He is present."

d. Fleshly Control

Our carnal nature hates surrender. It wants to stay in control —even in prayer. But listening prayer demands that we let go.

7. Cultivating a Listening Lifestyle

Listening and waiting must move from occasional practice to daily posture. You don't just visit this type of prayer—you live from it. Here are ways to cultivate this lifestyle:

- Set apart daily time to be still before God
- Fast noise—turn off media and let your soul detox
- Journal what you hear, even if it seems small
- Practice "listening pauses" throughout your day
- Invite the Holy Spirit to train your ears
- Stay accountable to mentors for what you receive

Remember: the goal is not just to hear something new—but to know Someone more deeply.

8. Fruit of Listening and Waiting

When you build your life around the prayer of listening and waiting, your inner world changes. You become less reactive and more rooted. Less scattered and more sensitive. You don't just know facts about God—you carry the fragrance of His presence. You will also grow in:

- Clarity – God's whisper will make your path straight
- Peace – Anxiety fades as you rest in His voice
- Sensitivity – You'll discern subtle shifts in the Spirit
- Obedience – You'll move with boldness because you've heard
- Friendship – You'll stop performing for God and walk with Him

A Whisper is Worth the Wait

You don't need more noise—you need His voice. You don't need more performance—you need His presence. The greatest gift you can receive in prayer is not answered petitions—it's divine communion.

The prayer of listening and waiting is not for the impatient or the proud. It is for the hungry. For the yielded. For those who are not content with religious routine, but who long to know the heart of God.

In the secret place of stillness, you will find Him. In the silence, He will speak. And one whisper from His mouth will outweigh a thousand opinions from man.

So slow down. Get low. Be still. And let the voice of the Lord shape your heart, direct your steps, and anchor your soul.

Activation

Set a timer for ten minutes of quiet. Ask one question: "Lord, what do You want to say to me today?" Write the first gentle impressions that come.

Discussion Questions

1 . *Silence in prayer is not absence but awareness—the space where revelation unfolds.* Why is stillness often harder than speaking, and what disciplines help you listen well?

2 . Describe a moment when waiting on God revealed something words could never express.

3 . How does valuing His voice above your agenda redefine intimacy in prayer?

CHAPTER 12

THE PRAYER OF WARFARE

BINDING AND LOOSING – DEALING WITH STRONGHOLDS – PRAYING FROM VICTORY

P rayer is not only intimacy—it is strategy. It is not only communion—it is confrontation. While many enter the secret place for comfort and rest, there are times when prayer becomes a battleground. The prayer of warfare is the believer's posture when standing against the powers of darkness, enforcing the authority of Christ, and advancing the Kingdom in hostile territory. This is not a prayer of petition—it is a prayer of power. It is not reactive—it is governmental. It declares, decrees, binds, looses, uproots, and tears down. It carries fire. It carries force.

Every believer is called to engage in warfare. You may not feel like a warrior, but the day you were born again, you were born into a battlefield. Jesus didn't save us to survive—He saved us to overcome. He didn't give us authority just to escape—but to invade. The Church was never called to be a bunker hiding from hell. She was called to be an army that storms the gates.

Warfare is not a sign that something is wrong—it's often a sign that something is right. You don't face resistance unless you're advancing. And if you are called to carry breakthrough for others, warfare is the price of that mantle. This chapter is designed to equip you to fight biblically, pray strategically, and win consistently.

Understanding the Nature of the Battle

Ephesians 6:12 makes a powerful distinction: "For we do not wrestle against flesh and blood, but against principalities, against powers, against the rulers of the darkness of this world, against spiritual wickedness in high places." Your real enemy is never a person. It's not your spouse, your boss, or your critic. The real war is unseen. It's spiritual.

The enemy wants to draw you into fleshly reactions. He wants to pull you into bitterness, offense, and retaliation. But you must rise above the natural and fight from the Spirit. You must recognize that what you're facing has spiritual roots, and only spiritual weapons can uproot it.

Satan is organized. He operates through layers of demonic authority—principalities that influence regions, powers that infiltrate systems, and spirits of wickedness that oppress individuals and households. But the good news is that his kingdom is already defeated. Jesus stripped him of authority at the cross. Our warfare is not about trying to win—it's about enforcing a victory that's already been secured.

The Authority of the Believer

Jesus said in Matthew 16:19, "I will give you the keys of the Kingdom of Heaven; and whatever you bind on earth will be bound in Heaven, and whatever you loose on earth will be loosed in Heaven." This is not symbolic—it's legal language. Keys represent delegated authority. Jesus gave us the legal right to enforce Heaven's rule on earth.

To "bind" means to forbid or restrict. To "loose" means to permit or release. These are governmental terms. We are not simply praying for God to do something—we are stepping into our position as Kingdom agents, declaring what is legal in Heaven and illegal on earth.

If Heaven doesn't allow it, neither should we. If fear, torment, sickness, division, or poverty are not part of Heaven's culture, then we have the authority to bind them. If peace, joy, healing, unity, and provision are part of God's will, we have the authority to loose them.

But authority must be exercised. Silence is surrender. Passivity empowers oppression. When you understand your authority, you stop tolerating what God never intended and start commanding things into divine order.

How to Tear Down Strongholds

Paul writes in 2 Corinthians 10:4-5, "The weapons of our warfare are not carnal but mighty in God for pulling down strongholds, casting down arguments, and every high thing that exalts itself against the knowledge of God..." A stronghold is not a demon—it is a fortified mindset that resists truth.

Strongholds are built over time. They are mental and emotional fortresses rooted in lies. Some are personal—like shame, rejection, lust, or insecurity. Others are cultural—like racism, idolatry, or religious legalism. And some are generational—passed down through bloodlines until someone rises up to break the cycle.

Warfare prayer identifies strongholds by the Spirit. It does not just treat symptoms—it targets roots. When you engage in this type of prayer, you expose deception, repent of agreement with lies, and replace falsehoods with God's truth. You break demonic contracts. You destroy mental altars. You liberate your soul and those under your covering.

You must pray truth aggressively. Declare what God says. Use Scripture to dismantle every lie. Say aloud: "I reject the spirit of fear. I renounce the lie that I am abandoned. I declare that I have a sound mind. I bind every generational curse. I loose the blessing of the Lord over my life."

This is not hype—it is spiritual warfare. Your words create atmosphere. Your decrees shift realms. And your obedience builds new strongholds of righteousness in their place.

The Role of the Armor of God

Ephesians 6:13–17 describes the armor of God—not as optional but as essential. Each piece is a revelation:

- The belt of truth keeps you grounded and unmoved by deception.
- The breastplate of righteousness protects your heart from condemnation and accusation.
- The shoes of peace keep you mobile and rooted in the Gospel, even in chaos.
- The shield of faith blocks lies, fiery darts, and mental warfare.
- The helmet of salvation guards your identity and renews your mind.
- The sword of the Spirit, the Word of God, is your offensive weapon—it pierces darkness.

These are not metaphors to memorize—they are spiritual realities to walk in. Warfare prayer is ineffective without alignment to these truths. Your righteousness, peace, faith, identity, and word life must be intact. Otherwise, you'll war in the flesh and wear yourself out.

Before you bind demons, bind your heart to truth. Before you speak with authority, stand in righteousness. This armor is not for show—it's for survival. Wear it daily. Pray it on. Live from it.

Weapons of Spiritual Warfare

Warfare prayer is not random—it is strategic. God has given us powerful weapons to enforce breakthrough. Here are some of the most effective:

The Name of Jesus – The name above every name is not a magic word—it is a legal access point. When you declare the name of Jesus in warfare, you are invoking the authority of the risen King. Demons must bow. Chains must break. Systems must shift.

The Blood of Jesus – The blood is your covering, your cleansing, and your access. Plead the blood over your mind, your children, your church. The blood speaks louder than guilt, louder than trauma, louder than accusation. It declares: "Forgiven. Redeemed. Protected."

The Word of God – Every declaration must be rooted in Scripture. The Word is a sword, not a suggestion. Use it to war. Quote it. Pray it. Sing it. The devil cannot argue with it.

Praying in the Spirit – Tongues are not just for personal edification—they are for war. When you don't know how to pray, the Spirit makes intercession with groanings. Tongues bypass logic and release divine strategy. Pray in the Spirit until you break through.

<u>Prophetic Decrees</u> – Listen for what Heaven is saying, then say it on earth. Don't echo the problem—announce the solution. Declare the word of the Lord with boldness and clarity.

Engaging in Territorial and Generational Warfare

Some battles are bigger than you. God may call you to stand in the gap for your family, your city, or even a nation. This requires discernment, preparation, and alignment.

Territorial warfare engages principalities that govern regions. These are ancient spirits tied to geography, culture, and bloodshed. They do not fall through casual prayer—they fall through apostolic authority, unified intercession, and prophetic action.

Generational warfare confronts demonic patterns passed down through family lines—addiction, abuse, witchcraft, infirmity, perversion. These spirits claim legal ground until someone rises up to renounce the curse, repent on behalf of their bloodline, and release the blessing of the Lord.

You don't need to fear these battles, but you do need to be led. Don't step into warfare God didn't assign to you. But when He puts the burden on your heart, respond with fasting, unity, and prophetic precision. You are not just fighting for yourself—you're fighting for legacy.

Practical Signs of Warfare

How do you know when you're in spiritual warfare? It's not always dramatic. Often, it's subtle. Watch for these signs:

- Mental fog, confusion, or irrational fear
- Fatigue that prayer and rest don't resolve
- Cycles of strife in key relationships

- Closed doors despite obedience
- Intense temptation or accusation
- Dreams of attack, snakes, or demonic symbols
- Discouragement right before breakthrough

When these signs emerge, don't retreat—advance. Begin to worship. Declare truth. Call others to pray. Anoint your home. Fast for clarity. Take your position and don't back down.

Staying Healthy in Warfare

You can't fight demons all day and ignore your soul. Many warriors become weary not because the enemy is stronger—but because their rhythm is unbalanced. Here are some keys to staying healthy:

Remain rooted in intimacy. Don't let warfare consume your identity. You're not just a soldier—you're a son. Let the Father refresh you daily.

Worship as a weapon. Praise shifts atmospheres faster than any shout. Use worship to recalibrate and cleanse the air. Fast wisely. Fasting breaks yokes, but don't do it out of legalism. Let the Spirit lead you into fasts that restore clarity and authority.

Stay in community. Lone warriors fall quickly. Have a team. Pray with others. Submit to spiritual covering. Guard your thoughts. Warfare often begins in the mind. Stay in the Word. Declare God's promises. Rest your mind and spirit.

Enforcing the Victory of Christ

Warfare is real, but Jesus has already won. You are not begging for breakthrough—you are enforcing it. You are not asking the enemy to retreat—you are commanding him in the name of the

King. The cross is your confidence. The blood is your banner. The Spirit is your strength. And the Word is your sword.

So rise up. Don't just defend territory—take it. Don't just pray for peace—command it. Don't just rebuke the enemy—displace him. Because you are seated with Christ in heavenly places. And hell has no strategy for a believer who prays from that position. Warfare is not forever. Victory is your inheritance. Fight from that place. Pray from that posture. And walk in that authority.

Activation

Pray Ephesians 6:10-18. Visualize putting on each piece of armor. Declare victory in Christ over one area of opposition you face.

Discussion Questions

1 . *Prayer is not only intimacy—it is invasion; the weapon that enforces victory.* What spiritual battlegrounds has God assigned you to fight for, and how do you war from victory rather than for it?

2 . How do worship and authority intersect in effective spiritual warfare?

3 . In what ways does fear lose power when you learn to pray offensively instead of defensively?

CHAPTER 13

BUILDING A PRAYER HABIT

DAILY DISCIPLINES – PRACTICAL TOOLS – PRAYING WITHOUT CEASING

There is no spiritual maturity without consistency in prayer. Gifts may be given in a moment, but depth is developed over time. The most powerful believers are not those with the loudest voice in the room but those with the deepest roots in the secret place. The habit of prayer is not an optional luxury for the spiritually elite—it is a vital rhythm for every believer who desires to grow, lead, and live in alignment with the purposes of God.

Many believers struggle with prayer not because they lack desire, but because they lack discipline. They love God but feel spiritually dry. They want to grow, but feel stuck in cycles of inconsistency. The truth is, prayer must be built into your life as a non-negotiable habit. Just as food sustains your physical body, prayer sustains your spiritual man. And just as muscles grow with repetition, your spiritual capacity expands as you engage God regularly.

This chapter is not just about inspiration—it's about construction. We will examine the building blocks of a daily prayer life, explore the tools that help develop consistency, and unpack what it truly means to "pray without ceasing." Whether you're beginning a prayer journey or seeking to deepen your rhythms, this chapter will help you move from sporadic encounters to a sustainable life in the Spirit.

The Power of Consistency

Consistency is what separates spiritual enthusiasm from spiritual maturity. Anyone can pray when emotions are high or crisis hits. But the true power of prayer is revealed in the day-to-day faithfulness to meet with God when no one is watching and when nothing seems urgent.

When Jesus walked the earth, He modeled consistent prayer. Luke 5:16 says, "Jesus often withdrew to lonely places and prayed." Not occasionally. Often. He prioritized intimacy with the Father even when He was surrounded by crowds, miracles, and ministry. If the sinless Son of God needed consistent prayer, how much more do we?

Consistency creates momentum. The more you pray, the easier it becomes. Your spirit becomes more attuned to God's voice. Your thoughts become clearer. Your emotions stabilize. You begin to carry a holy awareness that God is near. But this only comes through commitment. Moments of prayer are valuable, but habits of prayer are transformative.

Discipline Before Desire

Many people wait to feel like praying before they pray. But just like any habit—whether going to the gym, eating healthy, or studying—the desire often follows the discipline. You don't build a prayer life by waiting for inspiration. You build it by making a decision.

Prayer is a spiritual discipline. That means it must be practiced intentionally. You won't drift into a life of deep prayer. You have to drive there. The psalmist said in Psalm 5:3, "In the morning, O Lord, you hear my voice; in the morning I lay my requests before you and wait expectantly." He had a time. He had a rhythm. And he came with expectation.

Start where you are. If you're new to prayer, begin with 10 minutes a day. Set a time and space. Guard it like a meeting with a king—because that's exactly what it is. The discipline will create a space for desire to grow.

Don't be discouraged if it feels awkward at first. You are training your spirit. Keep showing up. The more you honor the appointment, the more aware you'll become of His presence. Passion follows priority.

Creating a Sacred Space

Your environment shapes your engagement. While God can meet you anywhere, having a dedicated space for prayer helps train your body and soul to respond. It becomes your secret place. A meeting ground. A war room. A sanctuary.

This doesn't require expensive design. It could be a chair in your bedroom, a spot in your living room, or a corner in your office. Keep a Bible, journal, and pen nearby. Light a candle. Put on worship music. Make it a place where your heart can breathe and your spirit can listen.

Over time, this space becomes holy ground. Tears are sown there. Victories are birthed there. Battles are won there. It may be simple in appearance, but in the spirit, it's a throne room. Honor it. Protect it. Return to it daily.

Using a Prayer Structure

While prayer is relational, not mechanical, having a structure helps guide your time with God. Many people struggle because they don't know what to say or how to begin. Structure brings clarity without stifling the Spirit. One effective framework is the ACTS model:

- A – Adoration: Begin with praise and worship. Exalt who God is. Magnify His name.
- C – Confession: Repent for sin. Receive cleansing. Be honest with your heart.
- T – Thanksgiving: Thank Him for what He's done. Cultivate gratitude. Remember His faithfulness.
- S – Supplication: Bring your requests before Him. Pray for your needs, others, your church, and your city.

You can also use the Lord's Prayer as a daily guide. Each line unlocks a realm of intercession—from honoring God's name, to releasing His Kingdom, to receiving daily provision and walking in forgiveness and protection. Whatever structure you use, let it serve you—not bind you. The goal is connection, not performance.

Developing a Morning Prayer Routine

There is something powerful about starting your day in prayer. Morning prayer sets the tone. It aligns your heart. It gives you strength before the battle and peace before the storm.

David said in Psalm 143:8, *"Let the morning bring me word of your unfailing love, for I have put my trust in you."* He didn't wait for the chaos to calm down—he started his day centered in God's love. Here's a sample morning routine:

1. Worship (5 minutes) – Put on a worship song and let your heart open up.
2. Scripture Reading (5–10 minutes) – Read a Psalm, a Gospel, or a passage the Lord leads you to.
3. Prayer and Journaling (10–20 minutes) – Talk with God. Write down what you hear.
4. Declarations (3 minutes) – Speak God's promises over your life, family, and assignment.

Adjust this based on your season. The key is consistency, not length. God honors what you make room for.

Praying Without Ceasing

1 Thessalonians 5:17 says, "Pray without ceasing." That doesn't mean you quit your job and hide in a prayer closet all day. It means you cultivate a continual awareness of God's presence throughout your day.

Prayer becomes breath. You whisper His name while driving. You ask for wisdom during a conversation. You thank Him while walking. You listen for His voice in moments of silence. This is how intimacy becomes lifestyle.

Developing a spirit of prayer means your connection to God is no longer limited to "quiet time." It becomes an ongoing dialogue. He becomes your first response, not your last resort.

This kind of prayer requires sensitivity, not striving. It's not about being hyper-spiritual. It's about being Spirit-conscious. When your heart stays tuned to Heaven, you'll begin to hear instructions, impressions, and divine nudges that guide your steps.

Overcoming Distractions and Dry Seasons

One of the biggest obstacles to a prayer habit is distraction. Life is loud. Notifications never stop. And your soul will always find something easier than stillness. To overcome distraction:

- Silence your phone. Put it in another room or use "Do Not Disturb."
- Keep a notepad nearby. When a thought pops up (like "email the plumber"), jot it down and release it.
- Train your mind. When it wanders, gently bring it back. You're learning to focus your attention.

Dry seasons also come. There will be days you feel nothing. Don't quit. Faithfulness in dryness prepares you for fruitfulness in the Spirit. God is working even when you don't feel Him. Show up. Keep pouring out. Your roots are going deeper.

Journaling Your Journey

A powerful tool for deepening your prayer life is journaling. Writing your prayers helps you process, remember, and recognize patterns in how God speaks. Use your journal to:

- Write what you're praying about
- Record Scripture that speaks to you
- Note what you sense God saying
- Track answered prayers and testimonies

Reviewing your journal regularly will remind you how far God has brought you. It becomes a personal record of your history with Him—a testimony in ink.

Building Prayer into Your Schedule

If you don't schedule prayer, it will always lose to urgency. Build it into your daily rhythm like a non-negotiable meeting.

Block time in your calendar. Set reminders. Design your life around it.

Some people find mornings best. Others use their lunch break. Some walk and pray in the evening. The time is not as important as the consistency. In addition to daily prayer, consider weekly rhythms:

- A weekly day of extended prayer and fasting
- A prayer walk through your neighborhood
- An evening of intercession with your spouse or friends

Your calendar reveals your priorities. Let your schedule reflect your hunger for God.

Forming a Prayer Legacy

You are not just building a habit—you're building a legacy. Your private devotion becomes the inheritance of your children, your disciples, and your spiritual sons and daughters. What you do in secret will echo for generations.

Let your life preach what your mouth may never say. Let your prayer life shape atmospheres, break cycles, and set a standard for what intimacy with God looks like. When you pass on, let it be said: "They walked with God. They knew His voice. They lived in His presence."

A Life Anchored in Prayer

Prayer habits are not about religion—they're about rhythm. They create space for God to shape you, fill you, and send you. When you build your life around prayer, everything else aligns.

Don't wait for the perfect time. Start today. Create the habit. Build the altar. Show up daily. And over time, you will become a man or woman of prayer—not because you prayed once, but because you built a life that never stopped.

You don't need perfection. You need persistence. God meets you in the place of consistency with grace, power, and joy. So take your place. Form your rhythm. And become a dwelling place for the Spirit of God—one day at a time.

Activation

Create a seven-day prayer schedule—set time, place, and focus. Ask the Spirit for grace to keep it and reflect on changes you feel.

Discussion Questions

1. *Consistency creates capacity; daily discipline sustains divine encounter.* What practical rhythms help prayer become lifestyle instead of emergency response?

2. How do routine and passion coexist without one extinguishing the other?

3. What mindset shift must happen for you to guard prayer time as sacred appointment rather than optional activity?

CHAPTER 14

PRAYER AND FASTING

WHEN AND WHY TO FAST – TYPES OF FASTS – BREAKTHROUGH THROUGH CONSECRATION

The combination of prayer and fasting is one of the most potent spiritual disciplines in the believer's arsenal. While prayer opens communication with God, fasting sharpens the clarity of that communication and intensifies the power that flows through it. Fasting without prayer is merely hunger. But when fasting and prayer unite, they become a spiritual force that breaks chains, opens gates, silences the enemy, and causes the heavens to respond.

Throughout Scripture, we see men and women who changed history through seasons of prayer and fasting. Moses fasted and encountered the glory of God on Mount Sinai. Esther fasted and saved a nation. Daniel fasted and received prophetic insight that shaped generations. Jesus fasted and emerged in the power of the Spirit. The early church fasted and sent out apostles who turned the world upside down. Fasting is not a side note in the Bible—it is a recurring theme in every major move of God.

Yet in our modern world, the discipline of fasting has been neglected. Comfort has replaced consecration. Convenience has replaced hunger. But if we are going to walk in power, we must return to the rhythms of those who lived surrendered. This chapter will help restore the purpose, practice, and power of fasting as a lifestyle—not just an emergency tool.

The Biblical Purpose of Fasting

Fasting is not about manipulating God. It's not a hunger strike to twist His arm. Fasting is about positioning yourself for clarity, consecration, and power. It is a voluntary choice to silence the flesh so your spirit can be sharpened. The purpose of fasting is:

- To humble yourself before God. Psalm 35:13 says, "I humbled my soul with fasting." Fasting brings your flesh into submission. It removes pride and posturing. It says, "God, I need You more than food, comfort, or entertainment."
- To increase spiritual sensitivity. When you fast, the noise of the natural realm gets quieter. You become more aware of what God is doing and saying. You hear His voice with greater clarity and respond with quicker obedience.
- To seek breakthrough. Isaiah 58 calls fasting a tool for loosing chains of injustice, breaking every yoke, and causing light to rise in darkness. Fasting is a weapon against spiritual oppression and stagnation.
- To prepare for assignment. Jesus fasted before launching into public ministry. Paul fasted before being released into apostolic work. Fasting positions you to receive instruction, mantle, and direction for your next season.

Fasting doesn't earn power—it releases it. It aligns you with God's voice and agenda. It's not about punishment. It's about purification. It's not about religious duty. It's about spiritual hunger.

When and Why to Fast

There are different seasons when fasting becomes essential. While you can develop a regular rhythm of fasting as a spiritual discipline, there are moments when the Holy Spirit specifically calls you to fast. These are often moments of:

- Transition. When stepping into a new season, role, or assignment, fasting clears your heart and mind for God's direction.
- Intercession. When burdened to pray for someone else, a church, or a city, fasting fuels focused intercession and breaks demonic resistance.
- Repentance. When the Holy Spirit convicts you or your community, fasting becomes a way to return wholeheartedly to God.
- Crisis. When facing impossible circumstances, fasting becomes a means of aligning your heart with Heaven and declaring your dependence on God.
- Warfare. When encountering intense resistance or spiritual attack, fasting weakens the flesh and strengthens your spiritual posture.

These are not rules—they are patterns. The Spirit leads fasting. He prompts it, sustains it, and uses it for divine impact.

Types of Fasts in Scripture

The Bible gives us several models of fasting, each with its own purpose and duration. The goal is not to replicate these mechanically, but to follow the Spirit's lead as you fast with intentionality and faith.

1. The Absolute Fast – No food or water.

This is the most extreme and rare type of fast, typically lasting no more than 1–3 days. Moses (Exodus 34:28) and Esther (Esther 4:16) both observed this fast in critical moments. It requires divine grace and should be approached with caution.

2. The Normal Fast – No food, water only.

This is the most common biblical fast. Jesus fasted 40 days in the wilderness with no food (Luke 4:2). Daniel and Paul also fasted in this way. This fast humbles the body and sharpens spiritual perception.

3. The Partial Fast – Abstaining from specific foods.

Daniel fasted by eating no pleasant food, meat, or wine for 21 days (Daniel 10:3). This is often referred to as the "Daniel Fast." It's powerful for longer seasons of prayer and consecration.

4. The Corporate Fast – A group or nation fasting together.

In Joel 2:15–17, the entire assembly of Israel was called to fast. In Acts 13:2–3, the early church fasted together before sending out Paul and Barnabas. Unity in fasting produces multiplied power.

5. The Lifestyle Fast – Regular weekly or monthly rhythms of fasting.

Many believers fast one day a week, such as Fridays or the first day of the month. Others fast several days leading up to each new season. These rhythms help keep your spirit sharp year-round.

You don't have to copy someone else's fast. Ask the Lord, "How would You have me fast in this season?" He will guide you.

Fasting and the Flesh

Fasting reveals how much power your flesh has over your spirit. When you fast, the appetites of your body rise up and protest. You discover how easily you've relied on food for comfort, entertainment for distraction, and routine for control.

This is why fasting is a holy confrontation. It exposes idols. It confronts emotional crutches. It reveals where your dependency lies. But more than that, it empowers you to crucify the flesh and walk in freedom.

Galatians 5:16 says, "*Walk in the Spirit, and you shall not fulfill the lust of the flesh.*" Fasting is one of the most effective ways to recalibrate the spirit over the flesh. You don't fast to punish yourself—you fast to train your inner man.

You may experience hunger, fatigue, mood swings, or irritability. But press through. These are the signs that your flesh is losing control and your spirit is taking its rightful place. The discomfort is not a failure—it's a sign that something is being broken.

The Connection Between Fasting and Breakthrough

Isaiah 58 is one of the most powerful chapters on fasting. God rebukes religious fasting that is rooted in pride or formality, and then He describes the fast that He chooses:

"*To loose the bonds of wickedness, to undo the heavy burdens, to let the oppressed go free, and that you break every yoke...*" (Isaiah 58:6)

True fasting doesn't just affect you—it affects the world

around you. It breaks yokes in families, releases freedom in cities, and shifts atmospheres in churches. It's not about skipping meals —it's about shifting realms. When you fast in faith, things begin to happen:

- Demonic resistance breaks
- Revelation flows freely
- Inner healing accelerates
- Bondages are broken
- Closed doors open
- Generational curses lose their grip
- Divine strategies are revealed
- Revival is sparked

This is not hype—it is the power of consecration. Fasting is Heaven's scalpel. It cuts away the excess so you can see clearly and move freely.

How to Begin a Fast

If you've never fasted before, start simple. Don't compare yourself to others. Don't aim for a 40-day water-only fast on your first try. Start with one meal, then one day. Grow from there. Here are some simple steps to begin:

1. Ask the Holy Spirit to lead you.
2. What kind of fast? How long? What's the focus?
3. Set a spiritual goal.
4. Are you seeking clarity, breakthrough, deliverance, or deeper intimacy?
5. Prepare practically.
6. Adjust your schedule. Inform others if needed. Prepare your meals or abstain from social media or sugar—whatever the fast involves.
7. Plan your time with God.

8. Replace meal times with prayer, Scripture, worship, and journaling. Create space to hear His voice.
9. Expect resistance—and press through.
10. You may face distractions, temptations, or even spiritual attack. Stay rooted. Let God carry you.

Fasting as a Lifestyle of Consecration

Fasting is not just an event—it is a lifestyle. Jesus said, "When you fast..." not "If." (Matthew 6:16). It was expected that His followers would fast. It was normal for the early church. It should be normal for us.

Developing a lifestyle of fasting doesn't mean you fast every day—it means you live with a heart postured toward consecration. It means your appetite for God outweighs your appetite for the world. It means you carry an internal altar of sacrifice, where you continually offer yourself to the Lord.

When fasting becomes part of your rhythm, you stay sharp. You become more sensitive to the Spirit. You carry less baggage. You move with greater authority. You discern deception faster. You hear God more clearly. And you walk with purity in a polluted world.

What to Expect After the Fast

The greatest fruit of fasting often comes after the fast. When Jesus fasted 40 days in the wilderness, He left the desert "in the power of the Spirit" (Luke 4:14). Fasting doesn't just cleanse—it commissions. It sets you up for an increase of power, wisdom, and impact. After your fast:

- Stay in the Spirit. Don't rush back into noise. Stay quiet. Listen.

- Watch for divine appointments and open doors.
- Write down what you received during the fast—insight, visions, Scriptures.
- Guard the ground you've gained. Don't lose it through compromise or distraction.

Fasting births a new dimension in your life. What you receive in secret will manifest in public. What you break in private will produce freedom for others. And what you consecrate now will carry impact for generations.

A Hunger That Unlocks Heaven

Fasting is not for the religious—it is for the hungry. It is not for the perfect—it is for the desperate. It is not about proving something to God—it is about positioning yourself for more of Him.

If you feel stagnant in prayer, fast. If you feel oppressed, fast. If you need clarity, fast. If you want to go deeper, fast. Fasting is the pathway of consecration, the invitation to divine alignment, and the fuel for revival.

You don't have to wait for a corporate call. You don't need a crisis to justify it. You need a heart that says, "God, I want You more than anything else." That kind of hunger shakes Heaven—and the earth will feel the impact.

Activation

Choose a fast suited to your capacity (meal, media, or activity). Dedicate it to seeking God's presence more than His provision. Record any revelation received.

Discussion Questions

1. *Fasting intensifies focus, weakens the flesh, and tunes the heart to Heaven's frequency.* How does fasting expose what truly governs your appetite and attention?

2. What breakthroughs in Scripture or personal history came only after seasons of fasting?

3. How can fasting move beyond self-denial into deeper communion and compassion?

PRAYING IN THE SPIRIT

THE ROLE OF THE HOLY SPIRIT IN PRAYER – SPEAKING IN TONGUES – SPIRITUAL EDIFICATION AND WARFARE

The Holy Spirit is Heaven's prayer partner. Prayer without the Holy Spirit is lifeless. It becomes mechanical, routine, and powerless. But when the Holy Spirit is involved, prayer becomes supernatural. He breathes life into our intercession, guides our words, reveals mysteries, and aligns our requests with the will of God. The Holy Spirit is not an accessory to prayer—He is the engine.

Romans 8:26–27 teaches us that we do not know how to pray as we ought, but the Spirit Himself intercedes for us with groanings too deep for words. This is a staggering truth. Heaven knows our limitations in prayer, so God gave us a divine Intercessor to help us pray beyond human understanding. The Holy Spirit prays through us, for us, and with us. He is our constant prayer companion.

This means that every believer can grow in the power and effectiveness of prayer—not by striving harder, but by yielding more. The secret to powerful prayer is not eloquence or volume. It is alignment with the Spirit. When you pray in the Spirit, you move beyond the natural into the realm of the supernatural. You become a vessel of divine utterance.

What It Means to Pray in the Spirit

To pray in the Spirit is not merely an emotional experience. It is a spiritual posture of surrender and communion. It means praying under the direction, inspiration, and power of the Holy Spirit. Sometimes it involves praying in tongues. Sometimes it involves praying in deep groanings. Sometimes it's quiet, sometimes loud—but it's always Spirit-led.

Ephesians 6:18 says, "Praying always with all prayer and supplication in the Spirit." This is not optional. It is part of our spiritual armor. In fact, it follows the list of defensive weapons in Ephesians 6. Praying in the Spirit is how we go from being clothed for battle to advancing in battle.

Jude 20 says, "But you, beloved, building yourselves up on your most holy faith, praying in the Holy Spirit." Praying in the Spirit builds you up. It strengthens your inner man. It charges your spiritual battery. You are not meant to pray only with your intellect—you are called to pray with divine unction.

The Gift of Tongues: A Spiritual Language

One of the most powerful expressions of praying in the Spirit is the gift of tongues. Speaking in tongues is a supernatural language given by the Holy Spirit. It bypasses your mind and allows your spirit to communicate directly with God. It is a divine mystery that edifies the believer and brings alignment with Heaven.

Paul said in 1 Corinthians 14:2, "For one who speaks in a tongue speaks not to men but to God; for no one understands him, but he utters mysteries in the Spirit." Tongues is prayer language that flows from the spirit, not the soul. It is beyond comprehension, and yet it is powerful in its effect.

Tongues is not weird—it's biblical. It's not emotionalism—it's spiritual empowerment. Every believer has the right to ask for and receive this gift. It is not for a select few. It is part of the Spirit-filled life that Jesus promised. When you pray in tongues:

- You bypass doubt and unbelief
- You silence the noise of your soul
- You align your spirit with Heaven
- You edify yourself spiritually
- You release breakthrough and authority

Paul said, "I thank God that I speak in tongues more than all of you." (1 Corinthians 14:18). If this apostle saw such value in it, we must too.

Tongues as Edification and Strengthening

One of the most misunderstood aspects of tongues is its purpose. Many assume it is only for public interpretation. While that is one function, its primary use is personal edification. 1 Corinthians 14:4 says, "The one who speaks in a tongue builds up himself."

To edify means to strengthen, fortify, and construct. When you pray in tongues, you are building your spirit man. You are strengthening your inner structure. You are reinforcing your faith. This is why tongues is such a threat to the enemy—he knows it makes you strong.

When you feel spiritually dry, pray in tongues. When you are overwhelmed, pray in tongues. When your emotions are unstable, pray in tongues. When you need wisdom, pray in tongues. It is the most powerful tool to stay spiritually healthy and alert.

Tongues as a Weapon of Warfare

Praying in the Spirit is not just edifying—it is militant. It is how we war in the unseen realm. When we do not know how to pray, or what to pray, the Spirit takes over. Tongues becomes a weapon that confuses the enemy and releases divine strategy.

In spiritual warfare, the natural mind is limited. You may not discern the source of resistance or the precise tactic of the enemy. But the Holy Spirit knows. And when you pray in tongues, you engage in warfare at the level of revelation, not speculation.

Tongues pierces the atmosphere. It silences demonic noise. It routes principalities. It shatters strongholds. This is why the devil fights this gift so hard—because it is a spiritual sword in the hands of the believer.

Tongues and Divine Mystery

Paul said in 1 Corinthians 14:2 that tongues releases "mysteries in the Spirit." These are not mysteries in the sense of confusion—but divine secrets that God is revealing through your spirit. Tongues is a way to partner with the mysteries of Heaven.

When you pray in tongues, you often pray ahead of situations. You intercede for things you do not consciously know about. You pray prophetically. You release angelic assignments. You prepare the road ahead.

Sometimes after praying in tongues, revelation follows. The Spirit will interpret what was prayed by giving you wisdom, insight, or Scripture. Other times, you may never know what you prayed—but the fruit will come. The mystery manifests in breakthrough.

Yielding to the Holy Spirit in Prayer

To grow in praying in the Spirit, you must yield. The Holy Spirit does not force Himself. He invites. He prompts. He stirs. But you must respond.

Praying in the Spirit begins with surrender. It means you are willing to set aside your pre-written prayer list and say, "Holy Spirit, pray through me." It means you allow groanings, tears, or tongues to flow without fear. It means you trust that He knows better than you do.

Yielding also requires faith. You may not always feel something dramatic. You may not always understand what's happening. But when you yield in faith, the Spirit begins to flow. And as you yield more, the river deepens.

How to Cultivate a Life of Spirit-Led Prayer

Praying in the Spirit is not a one-time experience—it is a lifestyle. It is cultivated through intentionality, faith, and practice. You can grow in this just like you grow in worship, teaching, or prophecy. Here's how:

- Set aside time daily to pray in tongues. Begin with five minutes and increase over time.
- Ask the Holy Spirit to lead your intercession. Let Him choose the subject.
- Journal what you hear or feel afterward. Often revelation follows Spirit-prayer.
- Play worship music and pray in tongues over it. Let your spirit rise in worship and utterance.

- Join with others in praying in the Spirit corporately. There's multiplied grace in agreement.

As you do these things, praying in the Spirit will become second nature. You'll find yourself praying under your breath while driving, working, or walking. Your spirit will remain connected to Heaven at all times.

The Balance of Tongues and Understanding

Paul teaches in 1 Corinthians 14:15, "I will pray with the spirit, and I will pray with the understanding also." This is the balance. We need both Spirit and understanding. Tongues is not meant to replace your known-language prayers, but to enhance them.

When you pray with understanding, you use your mind, your will, and your Bible knowledge. This is good. But it is limited. When you pray in the Spirit, you go beyond what your mind can grasp.

The healthiest prayer life flows in both rivers. You pray with understanding, and then let the Spirit take over. You speak promises from Scripture, and then release mysteries in tongues. This balance brings depth and breadth to your prayer life.

Overcoming Fear and Insecurity About Tongues

Many believers hesitate to pray in tongues because of fear— fear of sounding strange, of doing it wrong, or of not being "spiritual enough." But God is not looking for performance. He is looking for hunger and surrender.

If you have received the Holy Spirit, you have access to this gift. Ask, receive, and begin to speak. It may sound simple or strange at first—but keep going. It is not about eloquence—it's about obedience.

Don't let fear rob you of spiritual power. Don't let tradition silence your spirit. Don't let confusion hold back your breakthrough. Praying in tongues is for every believer—young or old, new or seasoned. It is a gift, not a reward. And it's time to unwrap it.

A River That Never Runs Dry

Praying in the Spirit is not just a method—it is a river. Jesus said, "Out of your belly shall flow rivers of living water." This is the Spirit within you. And when you pray in the Spirit, you tap into that river. It never runs dry. It never loses power.

In every season of life, praying in the Spirit will sustain you. It will lead you. It will protect you. It will empower you. It is the secret to lasting fire, enduring faith, and supernatural living. So yield. Surrender. Open your mouth and let the river flow. The Spirit is waiting. Heaven is listening. And your spirit is ready.

Activation

Spend fifteen minutes praying in the Spirit. Afterward, write any Scripture, image, or word that surfaces—treat it as God's personal encouragement.

Discussion Questions

1. *Spirit-led prayer transcends intellect, releasing mysteries and building inner strength.* What happens within you when prayer shifts from language you understand to utterance the Spirit gives?

2. How does praying in tongues cultivate sensitivity and endurance in warfare or worship?

3. In what ways has the Holy Spirit redirected your prayer focus while you were praying beyond understanding?

CHAPTER 16

PRAYER AND THE WORD

PRAYING SCRIPTURE – USING THE WORD AS A SWORD – PROMISES TO PRAY THROUGH

The Word and Prayer is Heaven's divine partnership. Prayer and the Word are inseparable. Where there is a deep life of prayer, there must also be a deep well of the Word. And where the Word is treasured, prayer becomes powerful. These two spiritual disciplines are meant to work together—not in competition, but in divine partnership. The Word fuels prayer, and prayer unlocks the life of the Word.

Jesus declared in John 15:7, *"If you abide in Me, and My words abide in you, ask whatever you wish, and it will be done for you."* This is not a blank check for selfish desire—it's a revelation of alignment. When the Word abides in us, it shapes our desires, purifies our motives, and empowers our prayers. The will of God is found in the Word of God, and the will of God is the foundation of effective prayer.

Prayer is not merely about expression—it is about agreement. When we pray according to the Word, we come into agreement with Heaven. We speak what God has already spoken. We align with eternal truth. And in that alignment, we find authority.

Praying Scripture: Declaring What God Has Already Said

One of the most effective and powerful ways to pray is to pray Scripture. The Bible is not just a book to study—it's a weapon to wield. It is filled with promises, principles, prophecies, and declarations that believers can speak back to God with confidence. When we pray the Word, we are not trying to convince God to act —we are agreeing with what He has already revealed.

Isaiah 55:11 says, "*So shall My word be that goes out from My mouth; it shall not return to Me empty, but it shall accomplish that which I purpose.*" When we return the Word to God in prayer, it does not come back void. It fulfills its purpose. It manifests what Heaven intends.

To pray Scripture effectively, begin by meditating on it. Let the Word sink deep into your spirit. Then turn it into a prayer. For example, when reading Psalm 23, instead of simply reciting it, say, "Lord, You are my Shepherd today. Lead me. Guide me beside still waters. Restore my soul." Take each verse and make it personal, declarative, and worshipful.

Whether in Psalms, the Gospels, or the Epistles, Scripture is designed to become your prayer language. The more you pray the Word, the more your heart and mind will be renewed. You'll stop praying fear-based prayers and start praying faith-filled prayers. You'll stop begging and start declaring.

The Word as a Sword in Prayer

Ephesians 6:17 refers to the Word of God as the "sword of the Spirit." This sword is not a decorative piece. It is a weapon for battle. When you pray the Word, you strike the enemy. When you declare truth, you demolish lies. When you proclaim promises, you dismantle fear.

In prayer, the Word becomes your offensive weapon. It is not just defensive. It cuts through confusion. It shatters demonic resistance. It separates soul from spirit. Hebrews 4:12 says, "For the word of God is living and active, sharper than any two-edged sword."

When you are under attack, don't just cry out—declare the Word. When you're facing a storm, speak peace through the Word. When the enemy comes in like a flood, raise up the standard of truth. Prayer is not just talking—it is fighting. And the sword of the Word must be in your mouth.

Jesus modeled this in the wilderness. When tempted by Satan, He didn't argue. He didn't reason. He declared, "It is written." That three-word phrase disarmed the enemy. The same strategy belongs to you. In every temptation, every trial, every season of uncertainty, you have a weapon—use it.

Promises to Pray Through

The Bible is full of promises waiting to be prayed. These are not wishful thoughts—they are covenant truths. They reveal the heart of God and invite us into agreement. To pray the promises is to declare, "Lord, do what You said You would do."

2 Corinthians 1:20 says, *"For all the promises of God in Him are Yes, and in Him Amen, to the glory of God through us."* The promises are already "Yes" in Christ—but prayer is how we say "Amen." It is how we pull the eternal into the now.

There are promises for healing, provision, peace, strength, wisdom, guidance, protection, salvation, and more. Each one is a doorway of encounter. When you find a promise that speaks to your situation, don't just read it—pray it. Turn it into worship.

Declare it aloud. Write it down and revisit it daily. Here are a few examples:

- *"No weapon formed against you shall prosper..."* (Isaiah 54:17) — Use this in prayer when facing opposition or spiritual warfare.
- *"My God shall supply all your needs..."* (Philippians 4:19) — Pray this over financial situations or seasons of lack.
- *"He was wounded for our transgressions..."* (Isaiah 53:5) — Declare this for physical and emotional healing.

God is faithful to His Word. He watches over it to perform it. But He often waits for someone to pray it through.

The Role of the Holy Spirit and the Word in Prayer

The Holy Spirit and the Word are never in conflict. In fact, the Spirit always moves in alignment with the Word. When you pray under the Spirit's unction, He will lead you to declare the Word. He will bring Scripture to your remembrance. He will guide your utterance with divine truth.

Jesus said in John 14:26 that the Spirit would teach us all things and bring to remembrance all that Jesus had said. This is the Spirit's role in prayer. He is the Remembrancer. He fills your heart with divine vocabulary. But He can only bring to remembrance what you have first treasured in your heart.

This is why praying in the Spirit and praying the Word go hand in hand. One ignites the other. The more Word you store in your spirit, the more the Spirit can draw from it. Your prayer life becomes a furnace of fire and truth, where Spirit and Word flow as one.

Practical Ways to Pray the Word Daily

If you want to build a strong prayer life rooted in the Word, you must be intentional. Here are a few practical ways to make Scripture the foundation of your prayer rhythm:

- Keep a Scripture Journal. Write down verses that speak to your season. Turn them into written prayers. Revisit them often.
- Pray through Psalms. These are Spirit-inspired prayers and songs. Personalize them. Speak them aloud. Let them shape your inner life.
- Use a Bible reading plan. As you read, pause and pray. Let the Word become a conversation with God.
- Memorize promises. Keep them in your heart so you can declare them anytime, anywhere.
- Use the Word in intercession. When praying for others, find verses that align with their need and speak them out.

You don't have to be a scholar to pray the Word. You just need to be hungry. God is not impressed with theological jargon—He responds to faith-filled declaration.

Breaking Through with the Word in Prayer

There are seasons when prayer feels heavy, dry, or stuck. In those moments, the Word becomes the breakthrough key. Scripture carries power because it is God-breathed. It shifts atmospheres. It builds faith. It releases light in darkness.

When your prayers feel empty, open your Bible. Begin to speak the Word out loud. Don't just read it silently—declare it with authority. You will notice a shift. The dryness will lift. The resistance will break. The Word is not passive—it is active.

Sometimes all it takes is one verse prayed in faith to break through a wall. Don't underestimate the power of a single Scripture. When it is spoken with belief, it becomes a sword in your mouth and a hammer in the spirit.

Keeping the Word Central in a Prayer Movement

If you are part of a prayer group, house of prayer, or intercessory team, the Word must be central. It keeps prayer from drifting into emotionalism or strange fire. It grounds intercession in truth. It keeps your focus on God's heart, not human agendas.

Open every prayer meeting with Scripture. Let the Word lead your direction. Train intercessors to pray the Word, not just their opinions. Build a culture where the Bible is not just referenced—but declared, sung, shouted, and meditated on.

When the Word is honored in prayer, God's presence is magnified. You create a dwelling place for His Spirit. You establish a foundation that cannot be shaken. And you build a prayer culture that lasts.

Word-Saturated Prayer Brings Lasting Fruit

Prayer that is saturated in the Word of God is powerful, effective, and fruitful. It moves Heaven because it agrees with Heaven. It brings transformation because it is anchored in truth. It grows the believer because it renews the mind.

You do not need to guess what to pray. The Bible is your prayer manual. Every promise is a doorway. Every Psalm is a song. Every verse is a weapon. And every declaration of truth releases Kingdom power.

So open your Bible. Open your mouth. And pray the Word.

Watch what happens when your prayer life becomes aligned with eternal truth. The same Word that spoke the world into existence is now in your mouth. Declare it. Believe it. Pray it through.

Activation

Pick one Psalm or promise. Rewrite it in first-person prayer form. Speak it aloud morning and evening for three days.

Discussion Questions

1. *The Word gives language to prayer; prayer gives life to the Word.* How does praying Scripture guard your heart from emotional or flesh-driven petitions?

2. Which passages have become personal weapons or promises through prayerful meditation?

3. How can the fusion of Word and prayer transform not just requests but worldview?

CHAPTER 17

PRAYING FOR REVIVAL AND AWAKENING

CARRYING GOD'S BURDEN – BIRTHING MOVES OF GOD – HISTORICAL REVIVALS FUELED BY PRAYER

The cry for revival is a Divine stirring. Every great revival begins with a cry. Not a cry from the pulpit, but a cry from the secret place. Not a performance before men, but a travail before God. Revival does not come because of strategies, programs, or talent. It comes when the hearts of men and women become desperate enough to labor in the place of prayer until Heaven invades Earth.

Throughout history, the fires of revival have never been self-igniting. They are sparked by intercessors who refuse to be satisfied with religion as usual. Revival is not simply a season of refreshing—it is a divine interruption of the ordinary. It is a holy awakening where Heaven breaks into time, and the Spirit of God reclaims territory that was lost.

God is always ready to pour out His Spirit. The question is— are we prepared to carry the burden of intercession? Are we willing to pay the price of prayer? Revival is not birthed by convenience; it is birthed through contending. It is a work of travail, and only those who kneel can give birth to it.

Revival Begins in the Heart Before It Touches a Region

Before God awakens a city, He awakens a man. Before He pours out His Spirit on a generation, He first finds a vessel in the secret place. Revival is not something we summon—it is something we become. Personal revival always precedes corporate outpouring.

Prayer for revival starts with repentance. It begins with surrender. It is not about asking God to move out there—it's about asking Him to move in here. Lord, start with me. Set me on fire. Remove every idol. Awaken every dead place in my spirit. Make me a carrier of Your burden.

When a person becomes broken for what breaks God's heart, the Spirit of intercession begins to flow. No longer are they content to pray for comfort or personal blessing. They begin to cry out for righteousness to reign, for sin to be exposed, for the prodigals to return, and for the church to burn with first love again.

The Role of Travail and Burden in Revival Prayer

The prayers that birth revival are not casual—they are groanings too deep for words. There is a spiritual weight that rests on those who are chosen to intercede for awakening. It's a burden that keeps you up at night, a holy ache that will not let you go until God answers.

The Apostle Paul wrote in Galatians 4:19, "My little children, for whom I labor in birth again until Christ is formed in you." This is revival intercession. It is not praying for something—it is praying until. Until Christ is formed. Until the Spirit is poured out. Until the heavens open.

Travail in prayer is the spiritual equivalent of a woman in labor. It is the holy tension between promise and manifestation. And just as a mother cannot choose when labor begins, so intercessors often find themselves gripped by the Spirit in unexpected moments. They weep, groan, and cry out under the weight of a divine assignment.

Praying According to the Promises of Revival

Scripture is filled with promises that reveal God's heart for revival. He is not reluctant—He is ready. But He seeks someone to stand in the gap, to remind Him of His Word, to press in until Heaven responds. Here are some revival promises that should shape our prayer life:

- *"If My people who are called by My name will humble themselves and pray..."* (2 Chronicles 7:14)
- *"I will pour out My Spirit on all flesh..."* (Joel 2:28–29)
- *"Will You not revive us again, that Your people may rejoice in You?"* (Psalm 85:6)
- *"Ask the Lord for rain in the time of the latter rain..."* (Zechariah 10:1)

These are not just poetic verses—they are prophetic invitations. God gives promises so that we might partner with Him in fulfillment. To pray for revival is to take these words and echo them back to God with tears and fire.

Historical Revivals That Were Birthed in Prayer

Throughout church history, every major revival can trace its origin to hidden intercessors. Men and women who chose to burn on the altar of prayer long before pulpits were filled or crowds gathered.

In the First Great Awakening, it was the hidden prayer meetings in New England homes that ignited the fire. In the Second Great Awakening, it was intercessors who labored in weeping over the deadness of the church. The Welsh Revival, the Azusa Street Revival, and the Hebrides Revival were all preceded by intense prayer gatherings that broke through the heavens.

In the Hebrides Revival, two elderly sisters, Peggy and Christine Smith, who were 82 and 84, were burdened by the spiritual apathy in their village. They couldn't attend church because of age and infirmity, but they could pray. Night after night they travailed, crying out for God to move. Their hidden intercession opened the heavens, and soon the entire island was gripped by the fear of the Lord.

What does this tell us? That revival is not about being seen—it's about being faithful. It's not about position—it's about posture. God does not need a stage to bring awakening. He needs an altar.

Birthing Moves of God in the Secret Place

Moves of God are not manufactured—they are birthed. And the place of birthing is always the secret place. Revival is not something that erupts from the stage—it erupts from the womb of intercession. God is looking for spiritual midwives who will pray until something is born in the earth.

This kind of prayer is not rushed. It is not based on emotion. It is sustained by hunger. A hunger that says, "Lord, we will not let You go until You bless us. We will not stop crying out until Your glory fills the earth."

Sometimes revival comes quickly. Other times it takes years of plowing and sowing in prayer. But the principle remains: every outpouring has a hidden prayer furnace behind it. No public demonstration without private desperation.

The Cost of Praying for Revival

Revival prayer is costly. It will cost you your time, your comfort, your reputation, and your convenience. It will stretch your soul and challenge your flesh. It will call you into nights of wrestling and mornings of groaning. You will weep for people you do not know. You will carry cities in your spirit.

But the reward is worth it. To see a generation awakened. To witness churches set ablaze. To watch drug addicts delivered, marriages restored, and the lost come running to the altar—we cannot put a price on such glory.

Revival is not for spectators. It is for intercessors. For those who say, "Lord, here I am. Ruin me for the ordinary. Set me apart for awakening."

Strategic Prayer for Regional Awakening

To pray effectively for revival, we must also pray strategically. That means targeting key strongholds in our cities. It means praying over spiritual gates, over church leaders, over schools, government, and families.

Ask the Lord to show you the specific demonic resistance in your region. Is it religion? Is it sexual perversion? Is it racial division? Is it addiction? Ask the Lord to give you keys. Then take those keys into the place of intercession. Bind what needs to be bound. Loose what needs to be loosed. Speak the Word. Declare the promises.

Prayer for revival should also include blessing the other

churches in your region. Revival is not about building your brand —it's about expanding God's Kingdom. Celebrate every outpouring, every miracle, every breakthrough. Pray for unity among pastors. Pray for laborers to be sent. Pray for harvesters to rise.

Discerning True Revival from Hype

Not every spiritual excitement is revival. Some things are emotional hype or manufactured excitement. As those who pray for revival, we must also discern it when it comes. True revival will always have the following fruits:

- Deep repentance and holy fear
- A hunger for the Word and presence of God
- Salvations, healings, and deliverance
- A disruption of complacency and comfort
- A re-centering of Jesus as Lord

Prayer must continue during revival, not just before. Often the enemy will try to hijack a move of God through pride, distraction, or burnout. Intercessors are not just revival midwives—they are also revival guardians. Stay low. Stay hidden. Keep the fire on the altar. Protect what God is doing by remaining in the secret place even when the crowds come.

A Generation Awakened Through Prayer

We are living in a critical hour. The darkness is deep, the deception is strong, and the systems of this world are shaking. But God is raising up an army—not of celebrities, but of intercessors. Not of performers, but of priests. A people who will cry out day and night, "Lord, revive us again."

You were born for revival. You were created to carry the burden of awakening. You have been invited into the holy tension of Heaven invading Earth. So don't settle for business as usual. Don't be distracted by what is comfortable. Lock yourself in the prayer room. Grab hold of the horns of the altar. And cry out for the fire to fall again. History belongs to the intercessors. The next move of God is waiting on someone to pray. Will you be the one?

Activation

Gather brief notes on past revivals. Pray, "Lord, do it again." Ask Him to start with your own heart. Write what He burdens you to believe for.

Discussion Questions

1 . *Revival is born in travail; awakening begins in the secret place before it fills the streets.* What signs show that personal revival has begun in a believer before corporate awakening follows?

2 . How does intercession for revival demand both brokenness and boldness?

3 . What would it look like for you to become an answer to the very revival you're praying for?

CHAPTER 18

BUILDING HOUSES OF PRAYER

PERSONAL ALTARS AND CORPORATE PRAYER
MOVEMENTS – WATCHMEN, INTERCESSORS,
AND PRAYER WARRIORS – SUSTAINING
THE FIRE

We are called to restore the Altar. Every generation is given an invitation to rebuild the altar. In times of spiritual decline, God raises up those who will not only pray privately but who will also restore places where His presence can dwell corporately. Building houses of prayer is not simply about hosting meetings; it is about constructing environments where God is honored, Heaven's will is sought, and the flames of intercession never go out. In the spirit of Elijah, who repaired the broken altar before calling down fire, this generation is called to restore what has been neglected and reintroduce the Church to its priestly mandate.

A house of prayer is not limited to a physical building or a formal gathering. It begins with the heart of a person who burns for God and continues into homes, churches, communities, and cities. When the altar is rebuilt, fire returns. When prayer is restored, power follows. And when God's people prioritize His presence, revival becomes inevitable.

The Personal Altar: Cultivating a Life of Consecrated Prayer

Before one can build a house of prayer in a corporate sense, they must first construct and maintain their personal altar. The personal altar is where intimacy is cultivated. It is the secret place, the daily meeting ground between a believer and their Father. It is here that identity is affirmed, burdens are exchanged, and spiritual vision is made clear.

Just as Abraham, Isaac, and Jacob built altars in response to divine encounters, every believer is called to maintain a daily place of encounter with God. The personal altar doesn't require a special room or perfect conditions. What it demands is intentionality, consistency, and a heart that hungers for more of God.

In a noisy and distracted culture, the personal altar is more essential than ever. It is the place where our hearts are recalibrated, our minds renewed, and our spirits strengthened. Those who maintain a personal altar become carriers of God's presence, and these individuals become the living stones God uses to build His house of prayer.

Corporate Houses of Prayer: Cultivating Sacred Spaces Together

When individuals with burning hearts gather together, the corporate house of prayer emerges. Throughout history, corporate prayer movements have sparked revivals, transformed cities, and shifted the spiritual climate of nations. From the Moravian prayer movement that sustained 100 years of nonstop prayer, to the upper room in Acts where 120 believers waited in obedience, we see a pattern: when believers unite in prayer, God responds in power.

A corporate house of prayer is marked by devotion, not performance. It is a place where the audience is God, and the agenda is Heaven's. It can be daily, weekly, or set apart for special seasons, but its power is found in the consistent offering of unified hearts before God.

These houses can take many forms—church-based prayer rooms, 24/7 prayer ministries, campus prayer gatherings, or intercessory networks. The form may vary, but the fuel must remain the same: love for God, submission to His Spirit, and unwavering persistence.

The Watchmen: Standing Guard in the Spirit

One of the key components of a house of prayer is the presence of watchmen—those who take their post in the Spirit and remain vigilant in prayer. Watchmen are not spectators; they are spiritual guards, positioned to see what God is doing, discern what the enemy is attempting, and respond with targeted, prophetic intercession.

Isaiah 62:6-7 speaks of watchmen on the walls who never hold their peace day or night and who give God no rest until He fulfills His promises. These are men and women who are burdened by Heaven, gripped with urgency, and relentless in their pursuit of God's purposes.

In a house of prayer, watchmen are essential. They steward the atmosphere. They protect the boundaries. They discern when to intercede, when to worship, when to decree, and when to weep. Without watchmen, prayer movements become mechanical. With them, they become supernatural gates of Heaven's activity.

Intercessors and Prayer Warriors: Birthing the Purposes of God

Alongside watchmen are intercessors and spiritual warriors. Intercessors are those who stand in the gap on behalf of others—

pleading, repenting, and contending for God's mercy and justice to be poured out. They carry the burdens of cities, churches, leaders, and nations. They weep where others are unaware. They travail until the breakthrough comes.

Prayer warriors, while often intercessors as well, focus on combat in the spirit realm. They take up the weapons of the Word, the blood, and the name of Jesus to demolish demonic strongholds, bind and loose, and enforce the victory of Christ in regions and circumstances.

In houses of prayer, both intercession and warfare are required. Some hours call for travailing tears. Others demand bold declarations. A balanced house of prayer makes room for both dimensions—supplication and strategy, surrender and strength.

Music and the Atmosphere of Prayer

In many modern houses of prayer, worship and music play a vital role. This isn't to entertain but to set the tone for divine encounter. In Scripture, we see that prophetic musicians often accompanied prayer (2 Kings 3:15, 1 Chronicles 25:1). Music softens hearts, lifts faith, and invites the manifest presence of God.

A prayer house that incorporates worship does so with one goal: to glorify Jesus. The sound released in worship-prayer environments becomes prophetic, penetrating the spirit realm, shifting atmospheres, and calling Heaven to earth. These sacred sounds create a rhythm in the room that draws others in and keeps the fire burning.

However, music must always serve the prayer—not replace it. In houses of prayer, music is not a performance, and musicians are not artists—they are Levites, anointed to minister to God and to the people.

Sustaining the Fire: Avoiding Burnout in Prayer Movements

One of the greatest challenges in building a house of prayer is sustaining it over time. Initial passion can launch a prayer gathering, but it takes divine wisdom, structure, and pastoral care to keep it burning. Sustainability requires balance between zeal and rest, structure and flexibility, spontaneity and stewardship.

Burnout occurs when intercessors carry burdens they were never meant to carry alone. Houses of prayer must cultivate a culture of shared responsibility, mutual encouragement, and spiritual refreshing. Those who pray for others must also be prayed for. Those who contend for revival must also receive regular personal revival.

God never called anyone to be a machine. He invites us to be branches abiding in the Vine. Resting in His presence, worshiping in freedom, and allowing the Spirit to lead are all necessary to keep a house of prayer alive and vibrant.

Training and Releasing the Next Generation

For prayer movements to last, they must be multi-generational. We must not only model prayer for the next generation— we must invite them into it. Children's prayer rooms, youth intercession teams, and student-led worship-prayer gatherings are essential for continuity. If we do not train others, the fire dies with us.

Mature houses of prayer make space for young voices. They mentor, empower, and activate. The goal is not to preserve tradition but to pass on a burning torch. Whether through equipping classes, prayer internships, or mentorship models, the next generation must be included, celebrated, and trusted.

When sons and daughters prophesy, and young men see visions, it is evidence that the Spirit is being poured out. Prayer movements that ignore the youth are movements preparing to die. But those who sow into the next generation will see a fire that cannot be quenched.

Apostolic Covering and Spiritual Authority

No house of prayer is meant to exist in isolation. While it may begin with a small group of burdened believers, it must be built with accountability and aligned with spiritual authority. Prayer movements thrive when connected to apostolic and pastoral leadership who provide covering, correction, and care.

Spiritual authority does not control but cultivates. It doesn't quench the Spirit but channels the anointing with wisdom. Every prayer leader needs a leader. Every prayer room needs oversight. This ensures longevity, doctrinal health, and spiritual safety.

A house of prayer under covering becomes a house with government. And a house with government becomes a gate of Heaven on earth—one that withstands the storms and bears fruit that remains.

Prayer and the Return of Jesus

Finally, it must be said: all true houses of prayer are ultimately eschatological. They burn not just for revival now but for the return of the King. They echo the cry of the Spirit and the Bride: "Come, Lord Jesus." (Revelation 22:17) Houses of prayer are bridal chambers where intimacy is deepened, oil is gathered, and the Bride is made ready.

As we build these houses of prayer—brick by spiritual brick—we prepare the way of the Lord. Our prayers are incense before His throne. Our worship is fragrance in His courts. And our longing for His return is the longing of Heaven itself.

Becoming God's Dwelling Place

To build a house of prayer is to say to God, "You are welcome here." It is to create space, build culture, and guard the flame of devotion. It begins with one heart on fire and multiplies into a community consumed with Him. In the end, the house of prayer is not just a room or a service—it is the dwelling place of God among His people.

Let us rise and build. Let us take our place on the wall. Let us cry out until He comes. For from the rising of the sun to its setting, His name will be great, and incense will arise from every place (Malachi 1:11). May our generation be the one that builds houses of prayer that touch Heaven and transform the earth.

Activation

Dedicate a physical space in your home for prayer. Play worship music, invite His presence, and commit that space to continual communion.

Discussion Questions

1 . *God is restoring communities centered on continual worship and intercession.* What distinguishes a true house of prayer from a prayer meeting or event?

2 . How can unity, purity, and perseverance be cultivated among those who carry the fire of intercession?

3 . What personal sacrifices are required to help sustain a culture of unceasing prayer?

CHAPTER 19

LEADING OTHERS IN PRAYER

THE CALL TO LEAD IN PRAYER

L eading others in prayer is not merely about being the loudest voice in the room or possessing an eloquent way with words—it is about spiritual leadership rooted in intimacy with God and a deep awareness of Heaven's heart. When someone leads prayer, they are not just initiating conversation; they are stepping into a priestly and prophetic role, representing both God to the people and the people to God. This sacred responsibility requires maturity, humility, discernment, and spiritual authority. In every generation, God raises up those who can lead others into His presence—intercessors, watchmen, pastors, and worshipers who help others encounter the King.

Prayer Leadership as Discipleship

At its core, leading prayer is a form of discipleship. When we teach others how to pray, model effective prayer, and create space for communal prayer, we are forming people spiritually. We are teaching them how to engage Heaven, how to commune with the Father, and how to contend for the will of God on the earth. Jesus' own disciples asked Him, "Lord, teach us to pray" (Luke 11:1), not because they didn't pray already, but because they saw a depth and effectiveness in His communion with the Father that was missing in their own lives. As spiritual leaders, we have the opportunity to be living examples of what a vibrant prayer life looks like, stirring others to seek God with greater hunger.

Creating a Culture of Prayer

Every healthy church or ministry must cultivate a culture of prayer. This doesn't happen by accident. It must be modeled, taught, and prioritized. Leaders who carry a burden for prayer must be intentional in building atmospheres where prayer is central—not just a side dish to the "main service." This includes pre-service prayer, prayer altars, weekly prayer meetings, fasting seasons, and corporate intercession for the city, nation, and world. Leaders must protect the value of prayer even when it's not glamorous. Revival doesn't begin on the stage; it begins in the prayer room. When prayer is honored, the presence of God increases, spiritual gifts are stirred, and a hunger for more of God is ignited in the people.

Teaching Prayer with Simplicity and Depth

It's important to remember that many believers feel insecure or inadequate when it comes to prayer. They may have grown up in religious environments where prayer was scripted or legalistic, or they may simply not have been discipled in prayer. Therefore, those who lead must be both pastoral and prophetic—teaching prayer in a way that is simple enough for the new believer to grasp, but rich enough to challenge the mature. Teach that prayer is talking to God, but also listening. That prayer is surrender, but also bold petition. Teach people how to pray the Word, how to sit in silence, how to cry out in travail, and how to worship in spirit and truth. The more people understand the multifaceted beauty of prayer, the more confident they become in approaching God.

Leading Corporate Prayer with Clarity and Authority

There is a distinct difference between praying alone and leading others in prayer. Leading corporate prayer requires clarity, boldness, and sensitivity to the Holy Spirit. Leaders must learn how to guide the people without dominating them, how to inspire faith without manipulating emotions, and how to flow with the Spirit without becoming chaotic or confusing. Clarity is key—beginning with a focused Scripture or prophetic sense of direction, giving the people language and targets for their prayers, and allowing room for spontaneous intercession. Effective leaders pray with authority, not because they are loud, but because they know who they are in Christ and they are praying from a place of revelation.

Equipping Prayer Teams and Leaders

As prayer grows in a church or ministry, there is often a need to equip and release others to lead. No one person can carry the burden of prayer alone. Leaders must identify, disciple, and empower intercessors, watchmen, and prayer warriors. These individuals are often prophetic, spiritually discerning, and carry a burden that goes beyond typical devotion. Equipping these individuals involves teaching spiritual authority, helping them grow in character, ensuring they stay submitted to leadership, and creating structure and accountability. A healthy prayer team is not a rogue group of intercessors doing their own thing—it is a unified, submitted force advancing the Kingdom.

Leading Prayer in Different Contexts

Prayer leadership can take many forms: a midweek prayer meeting, a Zoom intercession call, a Sunday morning altar time, a youth worship night, or even a street evangelism outreach. Each context requires a slightly different approach. In a more spontaneous environment, leaders may need to discern and respond to what the Spirit is doing in the moment. In a scheduled prayer gathering, they may need to balance structure with flow. In public evangelism settings, prayer must often be concise, bold, and filled with faith. Whatever the context, the goal remains the same: to connect people with the heart of God and to release the power of Heaven into the situation.

Dealing with Challenges in Leading Prayer

Leading others in prayer is not without its challenges. There are times when the atmosphere feels dry, when spiritual warfare is intense, or when people are disengaged. Leaders must learn not to be discouraged by these moments. Prayer is not always about what we feel—it is about what we believe. Leaders must press through resistance with faith, worship, and the Word. There may also be times when people become overly emotional, distracting, or even manipulative during prayer times. Leaders must lovingly redirect, gently correct when needed, and protect the spiritual integrity of the room. Spiritual maturity, discernment, and a spirit of humility are crucial for navigating these moments.

Raising Up the Next Generation of Prayer Leaders

One of the greatest responsibilities of a prayer leader is to reproduce. We must never become possessive or insecure about our role in prayer. Instead, we must look for the ones who are hungry, who are faithful, who have a deep love for God—and begin to pour into them. Teach them what you've learned. Invite them into your own prayer life. Give them opportunities to lead. Encourage their growth and speak destiny over them. The next generation of pastors, apostles, prophets, and revivalists will often emerge from the place of prayer. When we raise up others in prayer, we are shaping the future of the Church.

Sustaining the Fire of Prayer Long-Term

Leading others in prayer is not just about starting strong—it's about finishing strong. Anyone can host a prayer meeting once. Few can sustain a prayer movement for years. The key to longevity is personal intimacy with God. Leaders must pray when no one is watching, must cultivate their own inner life, and must stay rooted in the secret place. Burnout happens when people try to lead publicly what they haven't sustained privately. Refreshing comes when prayer is no longer a duty but a delight. Leaders must also remain in community, stay accountable, receive encouragement, and prioritize rest. Prayer leaders are soldiers, but they are also sons and daughters who must stay connected to the Father's heart.

Becoming a Midwife of Breakthrough

To lead others in prayer is to stand as a midwife for breakthrough. You carry the cry of Heaven and the needs of the people. You help birth the purposes of God on the earth. You weep, you war, you worship. You lead others into places they would not go on their own. This is holy work. And it is work that is never in vain. Heaven sees. Hell trembles. The earth shifts. When you lead others in prayer, you step into your God-given authority and become a vessel through which His Kingdom comes. Never underestimate the power of a praying leader. Nations rise and fall on the prayers of the righteous. May you be counted among those who lead others faithfully to the throne of grace.

Activation

Choose one opportunity this week to lead prayer—a meeting, meal, or moment with a friend. Invite the Holy Spirit to guide your words and compassion.

Discussion Questions

1. *Leadership in prayer is invitation, not instruction—it's modeling communion before teaching method.* How can you lead prayer in a way that imparts hunger rather than dependency?

2. What qualities separate a prayer leader from a performance-driven facilitator?

3. How does mentoring others in prayer multiply both intimacy and authority in the body of Christ?

CONCLUSION

A LIFE TRANSFORMED BY PRAYER – LIVING FROM THE SECRET PLACE

Prayer is not just a spiritual discipline; it is a divine invitation into God's very heart. As we come to the end of this manual, we are reminded that prayer is the breath of the believer—the lifeline that sustains, empowers, and transforms. The secret place is not merely a concept or location; it is a lifestyle. It is where you meet God regularly, where your spirit is shaped, your soul is restored, and your body is strengthened. Those who live from the secret place carry a fragrance that can't be manufactured—they release something of Heaven in every space they occupy.

Jesus Himself modeled this life. The Gospels repeatedly show Him slipping away to pray—not out of obligation, but desire. He lived from the overflow of intimacy with His Father, and His authority in public was the fruit of His communion in private. If the Son of God needed the secret place, how much more do we? The transformed life is not produced by activity alone but by abiding. True prayer anchors the soul in the presence of God and empowers it to endure every storm.

Becoming a Friend of God

Throughout Scripture, God reveals His heart to those He calls friends. Abraham was called the friend of God. Moses spoke with God face-to-face, as a man speaks with his friend. Jesus told His disciples, "I no longer call you servants...but friends." Friendship with God is not casual—it is cultivated. It grows through consistency, transparency, and shared purpose. Prayer is the pathway to friendship. When we engage with God not just as servants but as sons and daughters, we begin to hear His secrets, feel His burdens, and carry His vision.

Friends of God are trusted with intercession. They are not content to pray self-centered prayers but long to partner with Heaven. They weep for nations, stand in the gap for cities, and contend for the Kingdom to come on Earth as it is in Heaven. Friendship in prayer means we linger longer, wait with Him, and listen more than we speak. It is not transactional—it is relational. As we grow in prayer, we grow in friendship. And as we grow in friendship, we become carriers of God's heart on the earth.

Prayer as the Foundation of Kingdom Advancement

No move of God has ever occurred without prayer. Every revival, every awakening, every divine disruption has been birthed through the cries of the righteous. Prayer is the foundation of Kingdom advancement—not strategy, not charisma, not human effort. The Kingdom does not move forward merely by programs or events, but by men and women who know how to touch Heaven and shift earth. The Church rises in power when it returns to prayer. When altars are rebuilt and incense rises again, God moves.

In this hour, the Church must reclaim the mantle of prayer. It is time for watchmen to be stationed on the walls again, for houses of prayer to burn with holy fire, and for leaders to model lives of intercession. We cannot outsource our prayer life to a few

—we must all engage. From the pulpit to the pew, every believer is called to stand in the gap, to weep between the porch and the altar, and to release Heaven's agenda. Prayer is not the prelude to the real work—it is the work.

Sustaining the Fire of Intimacy

Prayer is not sustained by obligation but by love. Duty may get you started, but only love will keep the flame alive. Like a marriage, intimacy with God must be nurtured. There will be dry seasons, but dryness is not death. In fact, some of the deepest roots grow in the driest soil. In these moments, prayer becomes a choice—a declaration of faith that God is still worthy, still listening, still moving. The fire of prayer must be fed with wood: the Word of God, moments of worship, and the wind of the Spirit.

To sustain intimacy, you must protect your time with God fiercely. Turn off distractions. Schedule solitude. Guard your heart from busyness and offense. Learn the rhythms of grace and rest. If you fall, don't stay down—get back to the secret place. If you miss a day, don't miss two. The enemy knows he cannot stop a praying believer, so he tries to distract them before they ever pray. Break the cycle of inconsistency by establishing rhythms of intimacy. Let prayer become as natural as breathing.

Raising a Generation of Intercessors

One of the greatest legacies you can leave is a lifestyle of prayer that others can follow. It's not enough to be a praying person— you must raise up others to pray. Teach your children to seek God. Train your disciples to intercede. Impart the burden of the Lord to those around you. If we want revival to outlive us, we must invest in the next generation of watchmen. Prayer should not end with us—it should multiply through us.

Mentor others in the prayer life. Invite them to your secret place. Model what it looks like to wrestle, weep, rejoice, and wait. Let them hear your tongue groan in intercession. Let them see your tears for the lost. Teach them the power of praying Scripture, of waiting in silence, and of warring with decrees. Equip them not just with information but impartation. What you birth in prayer, they will carry in power. What you cultivate in private, they will demonstrate in public.

The Legacy of a Praying Life

You may never be known for your eloquence, your preaching, or your influence—but if you live a life of prayer, you will be known in Heaven. Hell will fear your name. Angels will be dispatched at your command. You will walk in authority not because of title but because of intimacy. A praying life leaves a trail of answered prayers, transformed lives, and divine interventions. Your ceiling becomes someone else's floor. Your private yes becomes a public breakthrough.

Heaven keeps record of every tear, every whisper, every groan. No prayer is wasted. Even when you saw no fruit in the moment, the seed of prayer is eternal. Like incense, your prayers rise before the throne and remain. Some answers come quickly, others take years—but God hears them all. A praying life is a legacy life. It changes families, heals cities, and marks generations.

The Final Call: Return to the Altar

The Spirit is calling the Church back to the altar. Back to the place of fire. Back to the place of surrender. Back to the place of encounter. Prayer is not a side room in the Kingdom—it is the throne room. And every believer has access. You don't need a title, a platform, or perfection. You need a willing heart. A heart that says, "Lord, teach me to pray."

This manual was not written to give you steps but to awaken your spirit. It is not a formula—it is a firestarter. May it ignite a passion in you to seek Him, to commune with Him, and to become a vessel through whom His Kingdom comes. The altar is open. The incense is ready. Heaven is listening. Will you return to the secret place?

Let prayer be your first response, not your last resort. Let it be the root of your identity, not just a branch of your activity. Let it define your leadership, your ministry, your relationships, and your decisions. When you live a life of prayer, you live a life of power. You become a conduit of glory, a carrier of fire, and a builder of God's house on the earth.

Final Words

This is your commissioning: to live a life of prayer that outlasts you. To become a friend of God. To walk in intimacy. To partner with Heaven. To stand in the gap. To birth revival. To carry fire. To build altars. To lead others. To finish well.

Now go—and pray.

.

About the Author

Tom Cornell is the Senior Leader of SOZO Church in Washington state, founder of Walk in the Light International and SOZO Network. Tom is married to his beautiful wife Katy and lives in the Puget Sound area with her and their three kids. He has been in ministry pastoring and teaching the body of Christ since 2008.

He has a passion to see the body of Christ moving from people with an orphan mindset to that of sonship; equipping the body to do the work of Jesus resulting in seeing the Kingdom of God manifested here on earth.